Today's Store Walk

Trends, Tips, and Tactics for Today's Food Industry

Dr. Russell J. Zwanka

Works by Zwanka

Today's Store Walk: Trends, Tips, and Tactics for Today's Food Industry

The ABC's of THC and CBD

The Store Walk: A Walk Through A Grocery Store in Today's Environment

Magic Mushrooms: Future Trend or One-Time Trip?

A Post Pandemic Store Walk

Pandemic Positivity: Turning a Pandemic into a Roadmap for a Positive Life

Food Forethought: 48 Healthy Food Tips for Navigating the Grocery Store

Simple Solutions to Make Customers Feel Like Your Supermarket is Their Supermarket

Ties That Bind: Inside the Extraordinary (sometimes knotty) Food Marketing Continuum

CBD Reality

A note from your professor

CBD Dreams

Public Speaking for Everyone

So, how do I do this Marketing thing?

Marketing in Today's Cuba

A Store Walk

Dr. Z's Guide to Grocery and Cooking and Cool Stuff Like That

Successfully Succinct Stage Speaking

A Marketing Manual for the Millennium

Category Management Principles

Customer Connectivity in Global Brands and Retailers

Requisite Reading for the Renaissance Retailer

Operating in the New Cuba

Food Retail Management Strategic Cases

Would You Shop Here if You Didn't Work Here?

Customers First. Profits Second.

About Dr. Zwanka

Dr. Russell J. Zwanka serves as Director of the Food Marketing Program, and Professor of Category Management and Food Marketing, at Western Michigan University, one of the top Food Marketing programs in the world. Delivering high quality curriculum and applied food marketing skills, along with the Food Industry Research and Education Center, Western Michigan University endeavors to work with the food industry to provide real time solutions; while also helping educate the future leaders of the food industry. Zwanka has previously taught Marketing Research, Personal Selling, Marketing Strategy, Food Marketing, Business Strategy, Global Business, and Marketing Principles.

Having spent a career in the food industry before teaching, Dr. Z conceptualized and formed the Food Marketing Concentration at Siena College; as well as the Food Marketing Track at the State University of New York at New Paltz. Serving as the Chair of the Food Industry University Coalition (FIUC), Zwanka works with other universities teaching Food Marketing, to help educate the future of the food industry. The FIUC is made in part by the generosity of the National Grocers Association (NGA).

Dr. Z is CEO of Triple Eight Marketing, a retail consultancy- helping food organizations re-align around customer lifestyle and orientation. Dr. Z has led the merchandising, marketing, advertising, procurement, and all customer engagement areas for multiple food retail companies domestically and internationally.

Zwanka holds a Doctorate in International Business from ISM in Paris, France. He also holds a Master of Science in Management from Southern Wesleyan University, and a Bachelor of Science in Psychology from the University of South Carolina. Never stop learning....

Dr. Z can be followed at "Dr.Z@TEM888" and www.tripleeightmarketing.com.

So, what's new?

Aren't you tired of talking about supply chain issues, out of stocks, on shelf availability, unpredictability? Should we move on? Recently at Target, 12-roll bath tissue was "Buy two packs, get a $10 gift card". I'd take that as a sign. Let's move on! Supply chain is important, but it's a bit like teeth: it's the ones you're missing that people notice.

This is a vibrant, innovative, guest-focused industry, and we need to make sure those roots are strong and being watered daily! Guests depend upon our companies to help usher in trends, address issues, and solve their basic needs- all while compelling them to branch out, enjoy themselves, nurture their family, and stay healthy. It's a big order! But, it's one the food industry has been good at, *been the best at*, for over a century! We've got this!

This book is about what's new, what's changed, how to improve, how to connect, and how to ensure our stores and our engagement is at the level expected by the guests.

This, my friends, is **today's store walk**! Enjoy.

Customers, Guests

The customers are at the center of everything we do. **The consumers** are also at the center of everything we do. The *customer* is the one purchases the product, and is our **guest**. This is the primary shopper making decisions for their family, friends, etc. Those who will eat or use the product are the *consumers*. Consumers have a different role. In a way, they are the influencers of the purchase decisions. They have needs, wants, lifestyles, and those needs translate (hopefully) into the choices made by the customers in the stores.

The *consumer* should be the immediate answer when asked *who do we need to delight, who do we need to understand, who do we need to take care of*! The *customer* should be the immediate answer when asked *who needs a simpler assortment, who follows a consumer decision tree, who wants an easy to navigate shopping experience*.

And, to add to the complexity, you are trying to earn their money and time at the same instant a competitor is vying for the same! Money and time are not thrown around wantonly. Yes, they'll spend $800 on an iPhone and then complain bread just went up $1. This is a book on grocery stores, not Apple stores. Apples, yes, Apple phones, no. *Some things we may never understand….*

The customer expects assortment from all over the world available at their fingertips, they'd like food delivered in an hour, and they expect full price transparency. If you cannot come to this realization, it's time to close the book, *literally and figuratively*. The customer wants to know "What makes you special?" *If you can wake up every morning and know exactly what makes you special, that's awesome!* It's a cutthroat, low margin, high turn business where every penny counts.

You. Must. Be. Special.

Ordinary dies when ordinary+ opens up next door. *Be extraordinary!*

Be our guest!

Let's start at the center of everything, the person handing us money, and make a determined effort to get back to where we were roughly....*anytime before 2020*. Remember that time, the good ole days, when those people in our stores, browsing our online offers, telling their neighbors about us, were our **guests**? Remember that? At roughly the same time we switched from calling employees to calling them associates or teammates, we switched from shoppers to *guests*.

Then, the rush of 2020 came in, we put up plexiglass, limited how many people were in our stores, had online delivery appointments that weren't available for months, placed rest stop bath tissue on the shelf to be sold, and it pretty much became an adversarial relationship between those providing the products and those hoarding everything.

Okay, memory lane stops here! Let's go back to calling those who *choose to shop with us* guests again. Notice I said **choose**. They can go anywhere, buy from anyone, switch retailers when they don't feel loved, and it's time to ensure the red carpet is out and awaiting our guests. Let's get back to using rewards program information to *reward* those who shop with us the most. Someone who spends the *majority* of their food dollar in our stores should be *greeted as they come in, should have a store manager come find them to say hi, should get a free turkey at Thanksgiving without any hoops to jump through, and should feel like they are part of the family*.

On top of that, the rewards programs and data can be used to **acquire** new customers into areas of the store they are not shopping, **trade up** customers not reaching the average basket size of the store, **incentivize** those who do not come back in as frequently as the average guest, and to **lock in** those who are too valuable to lose.

It's a mindset that recognizes these guests have choices in their lives, and are **choosing to visit you**, so should feel like they are welcomed, recognized, and invited to return.

What's going on outside?

External forces are always pushing their way into our business. As defined in most textbooks, external forces are normally not *controlled* by companies, but they demand a *reaction* by companies (they're actually called uncontrollable forces for a reason). We cannot control all sources of inflation, but we can help solve inflation for our guests. We cannot control government leaders and make them get along, but we can work to understand legislation and help translate its impacts on our food and consumer products supply. Easy way to think of uncontrollable forces? **PESTEL: political, economic, sociological, technological, environmental, and legal**

Political: most people cannot stand the political infighting. We've honestly gotten to the point in this country where no one can believe anything. It's sad! This is a great country, and it seems we're moving backwards. What the heck happened to doing the right thing for the country and its people, no matter your political perspective? **How does this impact the food industry?** Better question, how *doesn't* it? Stop drilling, input costs increase. Mandate minimum wage, costs go up at the same time as job hopping increases. Continue fighting and governmental regulatory agencies take their eye off the ball protecting our food supply, So, the answer? Politics influence the food industry **a lot**! *Solution?* Who the heck knows? I'd suggest get involved. If you feel there are anti-trust issues impacting you, then voice your concerns. If you feel regulation is anti-business, then voice your concerns. The fear is we're heading into a state of

12

Seligman's *learned helplessness*, where we feel nothing we do can have any impact on the result. Eeyore is a super little donkey, but that mentality is not how this country was formed!

Political: geo-politics and controlling of resources is a hot topic. In Maslow's Hierarchy of Needs, physiological needs come first, and you cannot advance up the pyramid until those needs are securely met. Physiological includes food, water, and shelter. Those things start to go downhill, and the fight instinct kicks in. Controlling food supplies ranks higher than even oil. Yes, oil is important, but remember how it felt when the mandates kicked in during 2020. The primary panic was around food, water, and shelter (and bath tissue). So, when a wheat-producing country is at war, or another wheat-producing country is sanctioned, there is global disruption. *Solution?* Well, there are a few. One, everyone could stop fighting….wouldn't that be nice? Two, and something that might actually happen, is work together on solutions for alternate proteins, alternate food binders, other methods of feeding the world, introducing farming to areas of the world that can support it and prosper. Many countries could contribute more to the feeding of the world if they just had an infrastructure in place to logistically bring their crops to market.

Economic: inflation has set in. Don't yell!! I'm not saying anyone likes it, nor would anyone balk at inflation going down. I *am saying*, though, most of us have adjusted our lives to inflation. Maybe drive a little less, eat out less, eat less proteins, eat more rice and pasta, etc. It's set in, and it seems we're all in it for the long-haul. Where inflation is hitting harder now is **inside companies**. Competitive forces have kept the majority of inflation from being passed on the consumer the first few years. Not anymore. At some point, there is too much pressure on the dam, and some of the water needs to be released! We're seeing this across the industry. Cost cutting comes in many forms: layoffs, freezing hiring, cutting travel budgets, etc. When that happens, uncertainty kicks in, and people favor austerity. When you're uncertain, you circle the wagons and cut back. You head towards private brands, etc. It's a vicious cycle, but is an inevitable product of inflation. *Solution?* We're doing it. Trim pack sizes, to make things affordable. Streamline budgets and operating costs, so your company runs with optimized efficiency. Find ways to automate. Yes, that impacts people. Yes, it also opens up new streams of employment. Remember the fact that every ten years, at least 40% of the jobs being done by humans didn't exist ten years earlier.

Sociological: our workforce is getting back to normal. The story of the last few years has been how multiple emergency supplements have lowered the motivation to work. Yes, there are a ton of reasons why workforce participation had shrunk, but one of the main ones was the social safety net. Yes, a social safety net is an important variable in a society. Also yes, workforce participation increases self-esteem, helps people feel like they are part of the solution, and allows someone to feel like they are a contributing member of society. We need a balance.

   Solution? Keep it going. Labor issues do seem to be leveling in most areas, except trucking. Focus on the employees. Remember, *pay is somewhere around* #7 in the list of "things most important to me where I work". Culture, acceptance, diversity of thought, embracing identities, being part of the solution, feeling like you have a voice. All are important. If you are in an office, **do not assume the "next generation" wants to work from home all the time!!** I go to companies with my students, and there's this misconception that everyone young wants to work from home. Absolutely not true! *Flexibility? Yes, of course.* Everyone wants that. The younger generation is actually starving to be part of the culture, be part of the team, experience work with people around them. This group was Zoomed out of a large portion of their high school and college years. *They do not want remote work!!*

Sociological: the workforce is shrinking. We *do need* immigration. All political mudslinging and blaming aside, we need a healthy immigration flow. It just needs to be done correctly. People looking for a better life, who want to follow the system in place for immigration, should be welcomed with open arms. Both sides of the governmental aisle have stated this as a fact in the past. The only issue is the narrative changes when the other party is in charge. I think we can all agree that healthy immigration adds diversity to our population, broadens our cultural perspectives, and shows we care as a nation. Plus, since this is a food book, the cultural influence of food is paramount to a constantly evolving taste presence in this country. We all need an increasing population. *Solution?* Let's keep doing our part on the food scene. A diverse culture reflected in food offerings is a great way to bring everyone together.

Sociological: speaking of immigration, diversity is in our DNA. A striking fact about the changing of the United States population: 21% of those over 75 years old are non-white. 46% of the US 18-21 years old are non-white, including 22% identifying as Hispanic. *It is expected 90% of the US population growth the next five years will be coming from non-white.* Look at your team. Do you reflect the future? Look at the stores. Does the assortment reflect the customer? *Solution?* As was said a few paragraphs ago, those who choose to work with us want to feel like they are part of the team and part of the solution. It's difficult to feel part of the team if the team looks nothing like you.

Sociological: living alone and unmarried is becoming the norm. People are either waiting to get married, or do not see the point. And divorce rate is at record levels. A single mom or dad, or a person living alone, has a massive shift in their expectations of you versus those with large families. Large families are not the trend. And, included in here is the "sharing economy", or the desire to not own assets, but to rent them or "borrow" (using an Uber is borrowing an asset). How that fits into your retail should be part of your strategic discussions. In some ways, even 16oz of pasta is too much leftover for a single person living alone.

Solution? Know your customer base. Not everyone wants club-size packs. Larger packs do contribute to food waste, when in the wrong household. Make sure to take care of those who still want a great meal, unique proteins, and a treasure hunt; but, they're not a family of five. And, it would help all of us if we could keep working to downsize produce packages. The number one category thrown out at home is produce. Shrinking the packages could actually lower the barriers to consumption, and increase inclusion from smaller families.

Sociological: speaking of living alone. Part of caring is *being watchful towards those who need help while shopping.* Have your staff trained to watch for an elderly person having trouble reaching things, watch to make sure the mart carts are charged and cleaned, go up and greet people as they walk in. The greeter at the door is only the first point of contact. Have the team go out of its way to greet the elderly. *This may be their only interpersonal contact the entire week, honestly.*

16

Help make it a good one! *Solution?* Most of us intuitively want to help others. It's part of the DNA of being in the service industry. The thing is, we need to pass this on. Wanting to help others can be a learned behavior. Leading by example is a super way to foster this mentality.

Sociological: why should I work? The generation coming into the most buying power has seen their parents "work until you die", they've seen people lose their minds over the stock market, they've seen illnesses and diseases because of overwork- and they don't want that. Do not interpret what I am saying as the next generation is lazy. The "work till you die" outlook has been replaced with "I want to enjoy and like my life, and make enough money to live well." Enjoying life's experiences isn't being saved for two vacations a year. Keep this in mind when hiring.

Solution? Sounds like a broken record, but encouraging a flexible work environment is the key. Even at the store level, keep in mind no one wants to be "on call". **No one.** It's like waiting for the cable person to show up. It sucks. As a lifestyle, do not run store operations in an "on call" manner. As a flipside, having someone come into work, then sending them home an hour later to "cut hours" is demeaning and wrong. If it's a snowstorm or hurricane, of course, those are extenuating circumstances. If you are always needing to send people home, that's a scheduling issue.

Sociological: the race to cities has slowed.
The city. Where things can be delivered to you, where you can walk or take public transportation, where all your solutions are within a mile or two. So convenient and appealing!
The city. Where you are crammed into little spaces, where you need to fight others for the "opportunity" to pay $3K a

month for a ratty apartment, where you could be mandated to stay inside for months on end.

The city is a conundrum. The race to urban life has slowed considerably, and that rural life looks kind of nice. The jury is out on cities. It's all about utility provided, and cities provide a ton of benefits. But, the cost is also high, crime is high, life is a hassle, etc. If you are operating in the city, keep in mind how important it is to have reachability, speed, access at all hours, a safe environment to shop, and something new every day. *Solution?* No real solution to be offered here, just know what you're getting into when you open stores in the city.

Technological: checkout free is NOT the future. I would have said in the past that we will soon all be checkout free. You just need the last generation that grew up with cashiers to move on. *I don't believe that anymore.* I firmly believe **self-checkout** is our future. Self-checkout gives you control, it allows you to watch your prices, it allows you to bag things the way you'd like them bagged, etc. Self-checkout is actually a decent experience, as long as you don't wave your arms too quickly and make the system think you didn't scan something.

But checkout free? No, I don't think so. **First**, for large orders, you need to bag your groceries and stores are not set up in "bagging order", as in you aren't buying the larger things first and then the smaller things. So, at some point, everything needs to go into a bag, unless you're Costco or Sam's. **Second**, most people just don't get it. For example, take some time and watch the "just walk out" stores at airports. Not only is *no one in there*, but it takes two attendants to monitor the just walk out....*two attendants*! Just give them a point of sale terminal and have them ring people out! It's not saving labor if it takes two attendants to be on call to explain to people the ease of shopping without registers. Registers those attendants could just run and make the store more inviting.

Nothing says "guests" more than making people walk through gated turnstiles, check in on their app, feel like they are being watched the whole time, and then feel kind of dumb when they are trying to exit the store. Checkout free is not guest-friendly. But, I can certainly see a time when *stores only have self-checkout.*

Technological: customers expect your mobile shop and in-person shop to be seamlessly connected. Whatever you offer and whatever you do, it should be seamlessly available on a mobile device. *An easy mobile interaction!* Make it as seamless as walking the store. Amazon has seamless interaction down to a science on their site. Those with more pronounced brick and mortar stores need to pursue seamless connection religiously.

Technological: using data to assist in lifestyles is here. Whether they are apps that form your shopping list for you based upon your preferred foods, apps that guide you through being gluten free or vegan, apps that help you find the best deals, it's all out there. This space could use some consolidation. It'll probably never happen, as intellectual property is a tough one to protect, as well as monetize; but still, there are a ton of ways apps can help. It might take a major retailer to use their app as a dashboard. This arena still needs to figure out where it's fighting.

Technological: AI is the talk of the town. If you haven't heard the discussion on artificial intelligence, it might be time to pick up the pace. This topic encompasses everything! Should we trust our future to machines, do we really want machines that can learn emotions, can machines negotiate better deals than human category managers, can machines order products better than human inventory managers, etc.

19

We're certainly in the infancy of figuring out how AI can, and will, impact our lives. In a way, we're evolving right now into accepting technology as our solutions-provider. We like it, it's kind of creepy, but the utility provided cannot be ignored. This one will be interesting.

Technological: 3-D barcodes are imminent. There is so much data available to be able to track sources of product, produce recipes, signal for recalls, etc. that the poor little UPC cannot handle it all. It's why so many labels have QR codes. 2-D barcodes encompasses UPC's and QR's into one delivery mechanism. 3-D is a way to make the entire package the data source. Just run the package over a scanner, *anywhere on the package*, and it rings up in self-checkout. Point your phone at the package, *anywhere on the package*, and a menu appears on your phone asking what information you seek. Like I said, this is imminent, and a necessary advancement for the industry.

Environmental: think ESG from the customer back. *Environmental, social, and governance* are not just words for the annual report. Think from the customer back to you. The customers really do care about the environment. They care about social issues and equity. They care about sustainable practices. And the younger generation? Even more. Tell your ESG story with a customer lens.

Legal: well, legal is so tied up in political, we're going to say they're lumped in together. Where our government can help in keeping our food supply safe, there is constant change. Labeling requirements, red and yellow dyes, naming salmonella a contaminant, etc. If you have a *positive* perspective on why things are legalized, then these moves help people. If you have a *negative* perspective, most moves are politically-motivated. I'd just choose to be positive. Life's too short.

Uncontrollable forces are many, and they have direct impact on our operations, supply chain, packaging, labeling, ingredients, etc. Being on top of these forces is prudent for any company in the food industry. The customers are counting on us to be able to interpret, understand, and then assist them in making their way through this thing called life. Let's move on to customer changes.

The Customer Changes

In this section, we'll do a deep dive into the customer changes hitting us. Customer changes can be anything from diet preferences, to shopping preferences, to food choices, to how they feed their families. These changes are not necessarily controllable, but I'd suggest we have more control over them than the PESTEL forces previously mentioned. Let's say we can *influence the paths* customers take to ultimately feed themselves and their families.

Limited Time Only is a strategy customers love. I'll always start with this one. LTO's are timeless. The LTO strategy adds *scarcity*. The customer will pay a premium just because they also want to share with their friends they got something no one else could get. *Scarcity works!* Tell someone there is a "limit of 6", and they'll buy 6. LTO never fails to awaken the competitive spirit in customers. We're all treasure hunters at heart, and discovering something limited in availability, that's the epitome of finding the treasure chest!

Upsizing is working. I'm including this one because it's counterintuitive in an inflationary time, but may products are upsizing, and it's working. From Oreos to Twinkies to lunch meat, larger packs in traditional stores seem to be working. Cursory feedback is that customers are visiting less, and want to ensure they have enough inventory, and they can read the price per ounce and see they are receiving value. And, if the items are expandable consumable, then consumption increases. It does make sense. Add LTO's to an upsizing strategy, and you hit gold! Just copy the Oreo merchandising strategy. It's a beautiful mix of seasonality, upsizing, thinning and then not thinning, LTO's, and shelf placement. Oreos! Nature's perfect snack!

Unique diets are the norm. Seaweed, onigiri, dried bananas, paletas, and even sea moss. Customers are pretty cool in the way they move around in taste and satisfaction. The key is to be there ahead of them. Vegetarian is huge (around $300B in sales) and growing, pescetarian (no meat, but will eat fish) is not far behind, plant-based and vegan are trending as well. Diets have changed based upon health benefits (or harm from what is being avoided) and/or climate and world impacts. The red meat methane issue has been discussed for years, but has gained steam. *Keep a vigilant eye on all diet trends.* They tend to come and go, but do impact sales when they hit. We're here to help, so try to stay ahead of what's next. *One tip: track vitamin supplements as the next food trend.*

Speaking of a story. *Customers want to know your story.* You are special for some reason. Tell people about it. Why should they care about you, your products, your store? People want to know you are run by real people and you have a story. Integrate that story into everything you do, and all marketing messages. Did you start in a farmer's market, are you third generation, did you raise cattle growing up, they are all part of your story.

Multipacks are the story of the year. It seems so simple, doesn't it? Multi-packs are having a moment. Walk every section in the store and you're seeing a proliferation of multi-packs with single-serve sizes inside. Snacks, drinks, alcohol RTD's, etc. It's endless what multi-packs are doing to drive sales. And, here's a cool one, include seasonal, expandable consumable, and LTO's in multi-packs, and it's a home run! Everything we talk about isn't mutually-exclusive. In fact, combining multiple tactics is efficient and can drive a ton of incremental sales!

DBA's: distinctive brand assets. With Pringle's, they are full of playful curiosity. With Hostess snacks, they fit a spot in the day: morning sweet start, lunchbox, afternoon snack, immediate consumption, and evening reward. "What makes you special?" translates into "why should I buy your product?".

Tired or Inspired. The customer who says *"I love to cook, give me cooking tips"* yesterday is the same one saying *"simplify my life and stop making me work so hard"* today. The best thing you can do is be prepared for both types of customers- **tired or inspired**. Offer meal kits and ready to eat for the *tired*. Offer ingredients, recipes, healthy ideas for the *inspired*. And be prepared for it to be the same person. It's a good issue to have. You're not one dimensional. If you were, you'd have bigger issues. You could be a mattress store....

We're all experts on diet. It's all at our fingertips, and heavily social media influenced. *Low carb, vegan, keto, paleo, vegetarian, mindful, flexitarian*, etc. are all well known to most customers. It would be helpful to follow these diets and offer the key components for followers. Talk about them on your social sites. Be an expert. And how about **chlorophyll water**, or **mushroom extract powder**? Someone in your organization should already be on top of it. Follow influencers. Real influencers, well....they influence. Many have masses of followers who will do anything they suggest.

Plant-based is here to stay, but....the interest level has waned considerably. Plant-based is settling into its own niche. That's about it. I wouldn't expect much more out of plant-based. It's been so highly exposed to not be much better for you, and full of sodium or unhealthy fats. Oddly enough, the main driver of interest in plant-based in the future could very well be the environmental impact of animal proteins. Watch for *plant-based seafood* to be introduced more mainstream, as why should cows and pigs have all the fun?

Conscious consumerism is here to stay. Yes, we are all conscious of environmental and social issues, plus health issues, and it plays into food choices. Understanding how the generations view consumption is paramount for food retailers. Older generations focus on *elimination* of ingredients like sugar and salt. Younger generations are focused on being *cause-based* or empathetic to growers, pickers, and workers along the supply chain. But, be careful not to paint a broad brush and assume these concerns are worth paying a premium. Yes, we care. No, we don't care so much we want to pay a 40% premium for the cause. Remember, our guests are loyal to themselves and their families first.

Olive oil, ginger, and avocado are everywhere. Remember when olive oil was for cooking only? Now, it's in coffee, it's a salad dressing, it's being deemed necessary to be eaten every day. Ginger is winning over turmeric. Maybe it's Moscow Mules, I don't know. In the race of the top trending spice, ginger is kicking dust in turmeric's face right now. Avocados are still raging. Just say avocado flavor, and the assumption is healthy.

Everybody is your competitor. Everyone is selling food! The growth of the **opening price point** and private label stores, such as Aldi and Lidl, has shown there is a market for this format for *all demographics*. **Convenience Stores** are selling more food every year, as consumers demand more accessible food near their homes- and tobacco use continues its decline. **Dollar Stores** that once sold variety items are selling more food every year, while adding coolers and freezers. **CVS** and **Walgreens** have gone way beyond selling drugs and related products. Many pharmacies have as many aisles of food as other non-food products. They are also adding coolers and freezers. And **Amazon**? Well, Amazon sells everything. The best navigator is the one at the top of the mast. Get up there and look over the landscape. Chart a course for where you're going.

Online ordering and delivery or pick-up. Okay, so not a change, per se. This one is with us for good, maybe with some tapering of demand. All the rage the last few years, for obvious reasons, this method of fulfillment is still set inside rigid parameters (order now, pick up or have delivered later in a window of time), which customers don't always like. Most of us don't do well with "periods of time" and scheduled blocks for pick up or delivery. Offer delivery and pickup, make sure you have built in a profit margin you are comfortable with, and that's it. Delivery cannot replace the smell of bread cooking in our bakeries.

Third Party Shoppers are annoying. At some point, the number of "shoppers" in the aisles shopping for other shoppers becomes quite annoying to those shoppers actually shopping for *themselves*. Plus, the nature of these services makes the fulfillers involved pushy and aggressive. And this goes for both third-party, like Shipt and Instacart, and our own personal shopper fulfillers. When speed is an incentive, it causes friction between those shoppers and the ones in the store shopping for themselves and making decisions at the shelf.

The solution for many retailers has been **dark stores**, or those stores operating as regular stores, but only for online order fulfillment. This trend started in the UK with Tesco, and makes perfect sense. Can you afford the real estate of having a store open, but with no customers invited in? I'm not sure there is a clean solution here, solely a point of friction between online and in-store. Same issue being encountered by fast-food and quick-serve restaurants. You have customers in front of you being de-prioritized for an order to be delivered or picked up.

Probiotics and prebiotics are surging again. It's not new to talk about probiotics, but the discussion has expanded to prebiotics, and the movement has expanded to the entire store. Where we might have just stopped at yogurt and cottage cheese, you can now add sauerkraut, kimchi, tempeh, kefir, kombucha, and miso to the list. Watch for this trend to continue growing, as the healthy bacteria in your gut and your microbiome continue to be at the forefront of health discussions.

Protein is a constant buzzword. Protein grams on packages is the norm now, and is driven by customer-demand. We need to work on helping the customer understand what it means to have protein in something. Many are pointing to macronutrient percentage as a better way to understand the balance between protein content and the content of other ingredients- good or bad. Macronutrient percentage measuring is coming to the forefront as a solid way to communicate balance.

Portable eating. Having all dayparts available in a bar form is not unusual, or new. But, the explosion of bars available for every "need" is unprecedented. *Hey, it used to be a Pop Tart.* Now, you have **RxBar, Quest, Larabar, Kind**, etc. The confusion that needs to be settled is where to place them all. We're a confused mess right now. A bunch of bars over in the *center store*, and a bunch of bars in *health and beauty care* (HBC). The customer has gotten used to finding their favorites where they find them, but that doesn't mean it's the right thing to do. Remember, we separate into categories and sub-categories so we can stay on top of trends for our customers. *When you're confused in the buying office, you're confused on the sales floor.* If it were me, they'd all move to center store. If you try to make a distinction between "healthy" and "unhealthy" bars, you're barking up the wrong tree. What is healthy is a personal question.

Frozen foods are rocking! A major uptick in sales the last few years has not abated. Frozen foods manufacturers have worked hard to reduce sodium content, and seriously offer a healthy alternative to ensure there are certain items in households that would otherwise spoil too quickly or couldn't travel to that area in a "fresh" state. Keep on top of frozen sales, as they are with us for a while. Everything in the store is offered in a frozen state, so maintaining the trends from the center store is imperative in frozen assortment. Some de-sku'ing in the "diet" section could help alleviate some of the space pressure. There are soooooooo many diet brands, and they each have appetizers, main meals, desserts, etc. You can probably choose one or two, and de-sku the rest.

Cannabis products and hemp-derived Cannabidiol, Cannabigerol, and Cannabinol. As a natural way to ward off viruses and diseases, the products derived from the *cannabis plant* (or the hemp plant) are coming into their own. If you've read any of my previous books on Cannabidiol (CBD) (see my book *The ABC's of THC and CBD*), you have read the vast array of positive benefits your body can see from hemp-derived CBD, including sleep, reduced inflammation, etc. In fact, if we could just fix sleep for people, we could cure a lot of issues! Now, add the federal legalization of cannabis products, and this trend is set to explode again. Watch for CBD-infused everything in our future.

Mushrooms are everywhere. Oh wow, what a trend! **Mushroom coffee, mushroom mixes, anything containing lion's mane, cordyceps, reishi, shitake, chaga**, etc. are all the rage. Most have not been verified to do anything for you by the FDA, but that never stopped a trend before, did it?

Food as medicine. Aggregating everything we've said about ginger, and spices, and mushrooms, and protein, and CBD, customers are coming to the realization that food can either hurt us or help us, healthwise. There's very little neutrality in foods, and many customers are overtly looking to food as a solution for health issues. We can play a big part in this arena, and be part of the solution!

Local and Regional are still hot. Everything from local foods to regional tastes, the desire to "support local", as well as the assumption that local means healthier (maybe not a fact-based assumption, but an assumption either way), is still trending. Look for the expansion outside produce to *meats, sauces, condiments, and bakeries* to continue. And if you don't already have a *local honey* program, it's time to pick up the pace on that one!

The neatest thing about the food industry is the *constantly changing customer*. The most difficult thing about this industry is the *constantly changing customer*. Keeping up with, then being ahead of, the customers is a full-time job. The best do it naturally through customer engagement at all levels, and a constant overt focus on understanding customer trends and being multiple steps ahead.

Customer demands from the food industry are higher than ever! High assortment, friendly associates, and bright beautiful stores. **It's a super mix of utility and experience!**

The Walk

Let's walk today's store! We're going to go aisle by aisle and category by category and talk about trends, the experience, value-seeking tips, cooking tips, etc. If you're in this industry, you love walking stores, and the next section of this book is all about what you'll find in today's store. **Let's get walking!**

The Entrance

You drive up, park and walk right into the store with your head down, right? Right? *Nope.* You know, the **outside of the store** can be as important as the inside. The outside sets a tone. It can be a *value* tone, a *seasonal* tone, or even a "we don't care about you" tone. Most of us get out of our car and look around. It's one of the reasons the fronts of stores look so majestic. You are entering a beautiful bastion of bounty, and the front needs to look like a castle. Uniform, clean, all lights in signs working, all lights in the parking lot working. Really, you shouldn't be able to enter your store for even one day if there is a light out in your parking lot or in your store sign. It's the first impression!

You get out of your car, and what do you see? A beautiful display of flowers, plants, and lawn items. What do you think? *Fresh, summer or spring, lively, beautiful.* That's the tone. You sell *food* and it's *fresh*. Food comes from the earth (mostly), and you can trust this store.

Now, what if you get out of your car and you see a massive truck trailer with pallets and pallets of paper towels and tissue on it, and a big sign for a great price? What's your interpretation of the retailer's message? *Value, price, best deal in town, get it while it's hot!* In both scenarios, your trip through the rest of the store? Same impression. The fresh outside makes the store fresh inside. Value and price outside? Same result.

Now flip the scenario. What happens when you drive up to the store and must get out and move a shopping cart to get into a parking place? Add that cart to the hundreds that are out in the parking lot, dodge a flying piece of debris as you get out of your car, and walk quickly past the employee smoking by the propane cylinders (it's happened, don't laugh), to get into the store. Now, what's your impression? Yup, this is a pretty easy one. This store doesn't care about *you*. They think you are fine with an un-safe environment that is wrought with peril. And that's how you're going to feel as you shop in that store. The outside makes a difference. You might want to skip the sushi in this store.

We've parked, are walking in, and the outside has met whatever expectation we have for the store. We slip through the sliding glass doors as they welcome us as only sliding glass doors can welcome us- come on in, stay a while! You walk into what we like to call the **De-compression Zone.** That big bad outside world was nipping at your heels, but here you are. A cool collection of some of the world's best food products grown or made by some of the most skilled artisans in the world. Take a deep breath….de-compress. *Big hug!*

What's the first thing you see? What's the first thing you should see? Let me introduce you to one of my favorite phrases- *It depends*. What should you see? It depends. If you're a value format like Walmart or Target, then you should see **value**. If you're a traditional format like Kroger or Meijer, then show off what makes you different. Go for **fresh**. If you're a club store, like Sam's or Costco, you start with **treasure hunt** on one side and electronics in the other side- all leading you to the treasure island in the middle. Brand expectations should be met at every step along the way. Remember, what makes you special?

Thank you for the hug. Let's keep walking.

The Floral

Picture walking through a wall of beautiful **flowers** and **plants** as you head into the most *luscious bountiful produce department ever*! Yeah, that is a beautiful picture. Every store should have floral at the front. It's on no one's list, except for Valentine's Day, and is a perfect upsell for every customer. Fresh sells in floral. Dark floral departments in the back of the store might as well be stacks of bath tissue. There's no upselling going on, so just give up. Bury it, they're dead.

But, a well-run floral department at the beginning of the store? *Call me fresh, baby!* Get someone to run your floral departments who is the most passionate and effusive person in the store or in the company. Really, that person will make your floral departments resemble their passion. Floral calls for *flamboyant leadership*. Seriously, find someone a little crazy and energetic. That person.

Some other tips, have the correct mix of **plants and flowers and bouquets**. Make it known you can make any arrangement or corsage or centerpiece on demand. The only other section of the store that demands this much artistry, personal touch, and love is cake decorating.

A few more hints, always have the $10 to $15 **bouquets in water buckets by the registers**. The registers are perfect for that last impulse buy of flowers. And make sure you have the bouquet dry bags connected to the displays. *They're wet, you know.* Now, how else do you get someone's attention? **Balloons!** Balloons! What is more attention-getting than a bunch of balloons? Have them on the flowers, have them in floral, have them near the special occasion cakes in the bakery.

Inflation Tips: *To assist in combatting inflation, many have turned to growing their own herbs and some vegetables at home. Make sure you have small plants, as well as seeds. You're helping customers, and you really should be the only place customers think of when it comes to food. Sorry, Home Depot and Lowe's, food should come from a food store. Play up the savings that can had by growing your own food at home.*

The Farmstand

If you call your produce department the **farmstand**, you're already winning! It's how you cultivate the idea of being in touch with the earth in produce. *It's a mindset.*

Ask customers why they choose their favorite store, and **produce** is almost always number one. Even the mass merchants understand how important produce is to keeping a customer returning. What makes a great produce department? Start with the *first look*. What do you see? Does it scream "fresh picked", "good for you", "straight from the earth", "trust"? If so, then good, *you're in the right place*. A beautiful and fresh produce department should delight your eyes and make you feel like you're at one with the earth. Seriously, that's how important the produce department is to customers.

Even the table or fixtures should scream earthy or fresh or "straight from the field". The fixture is there to **showcase the product**, not the other way around. To complete the ambience, there should be lighting directly on the beautiful produce (even dimmed on the aisles, to showcase the product even more), and special floors that are different from the rest of the store. An earthy wooden floor is a perfect complement to a produce department.

Let's talk **navigation**. A customer has an expectation to be able to walk around your department and *take their time* to pick out their produce. They'll also want to know who grew it, is it local, etc.? Make sure you give the customers *spacing*! The common aisle spacing thought is to give space to HBC and "personal" items, but customers also want to be able to make a thoughtful decision in produce, as well. Make the aisles wide and clean, and let them think! They're running through their food needs for the week. Give them a chance!

So, what's new in produce? The newest trending area is the **ready to eat** section. Normally reserved for deli, ready to eat is popping up all over the store. We're "back to normal", being rushed and not wanting to spend a ton of time on meal prep all the time. The margin you can make in ready to eat salads is off the charts, as long as you order and rotate it properly. Add to that, ready cut vegetables and fruits. Make it easier to consume produce, and the guests will appreciate the effort.

Bagged salads, usually adjacent to ready to eat salads, are not new, but have been holding strong. Make sure this section reflects new combinations of greens, and is also rotated properly. These bagged (or plastic container) salads have extremely close dating, and they need to move out of your store as quickly as they came in!

Seasonality is obviously key in the produce department. If that is new news to you, then kindly close this book and use it as a drink coaster, please....it's not going to help. Let's talk about product layout in produce. The seasonal part is the most obvious: apples in the fall, local corn mid-July, etc. The only thing that makes it seasonal is that one, the customers think mostly of apples in the fall; and, two, the sourcing moves closer to the store.

On that second part, please remember there are *apple customers year round*. Demand might shift a bit, but you still need a base assortment of those items you call seasonal. You just get them from somewhere in the world that is still growing and harvesting the product. I'm convinced that is why we have two hemispheres- *when one takes a break, the other one picks up the slack*.

As we discussed at the beginning of the book, **local** is trending even higher than it was already trending- and it was already strong! Remember, all produce is local to somewhere, so this is a balancing act. You want to play up local, show your local growers, but do not ignore great items solely because they don't fit a rigid definition of local arbitrarily determined by drawing a circle on the map around your store. If you followed that map unwaveringly, you'd have a boring department and risk being constantly out of items customers want. As with everything, don't rank *your* definition of value over the *customer's* definition.

Seasonal items towards the front, then break out into stone fruits (those with pits or seeds), other fruits, cooking vegetables, regular vegetables, greens and then bagged salads, and the green wall! **A green wall!** Now that's a differentiator! Angled almost vertically, the green wall makes or breaks your produce department. It yells freshness, earthy, healthy, wellness, fit, etc. It's all about the green wall. Look at Whole Foods- they know how to do a green wall.

What about stocky items like **potatoes, carrots, stewing vegetables**, etc.? They are bulky and, frankly, not very exciting. You need to ensure you have variety and sizes for all customers. As more customers have started cooking, look for this section to have a nice expansion trend. Vegetables are back!

And the "extra" section with **kombucha, live probiotics, pomegranate juice, immunity shots, and everything superberry?** Yeah, that's a big part of the department. If you're not focusing on these trendy items, you are missing a whole segment of the population that likes to "juice" (as a verb). Everything is now available in liquid form. Make sure you have the full variety. They started in produce, but now superfood beverages are everywhere! There really isn't a healthy food group that isn't also available in liquid form.

Organic produce. Organic is the growth trend of the

last four years and shows no slowing at all. This one area, along with local, is going to carry produce growth for the next five years. Please, please, please do not treat organic items as "we carry them when we have them". Make sure they are part of the set and are a mandatory part of the minimum assortment. In the produce department, it's best to have an organic section separate from the rest, simply because it showcases variety better when all grouped together. Plus, you can show a keen focus on maintaining organic assortment when you have a plan for all commodities in the organic section.

Just make sure the customers can find it. Maybe even put it first in the traffic line. Or, if you have a wide and spread out department, go ahead and place organic sections closer to their non-organic friends. Have an organic potato section adjacent to potatoes. Have the carrots and celery near the other carrots and celery. Just call it out big and bold! Customers *are* looking for organic.

A tip….for **cut fruit and vegetables, "loose" nuts and seeds**, etc., procure them from a producer who is skilled in manufacturing these items in a hyper hygienic environment! You cannot replicate these clean environments in a store, and someone's going to get sick! Go tour one of these facilities, and you'll see what I mean. I'm talking full body suits and walking through a sanitary mister. **That clean!** Anything someone picks out of the canister and immediately eats needs to be produced in a highly sanitary environment.

Carry sizes that encourage **full consumption** of the products at home. At least 30% of all produce is thrown away at home, and we can help. Shrink some of the pack sizes. No, offering individual fruits and vegetables is not the only, or best, solution. Bagged produce is easier to shop, easier to checkout, easier to bring home, and easier to consume.

Lastly in produce, what about pricing? *Price is not a*

differentiator. Repeat after me- not a differentiator. If people shop in your stores because of price, it's because that's all you have to offer them. Yes, price operators have something to offer besides price, but not much. The reason they exist is because of price. Unless you work in this price-oriented format, make it about the product- variety, service, cleanliness, customer service. Make it about the experience.

One thing on produce pricing, make sure you know the key items people will notice. Number one? Yup, you guessed it- **bananas**. One of the most noticeable prices in the store. Keep regular bananas at a highly competitive price without losing money. How do you make up the margin? *Expand your offering on organic bananas*, and make them competitively priced. The only way the math works on competitive banana pricing is if you offer competitive organic pricing and can increase those sales.

And, while we're at it, self-checkout is a major part of the future of shopping. The more you can do in the produce department to *help the customer ring up their produce easier at the front*, the better off you'll be. Plus, the more you can distinguish organic produce from non-organic, the more likely you'll be to have the organic produce rung through as organic by the customer.

For the rest of produce pricing, just keep it competitive. People eat produce for health, for beauty, for just about everything except price. Everyone knows healthy items are more expensive. Giving it away makes no sense.

Inflation Tips: You may want to try pushing the "ugly produce tastes better" program again. First, so you don't keep throwing away ready to eat fruits and vegetables, but second so you can offer an affordable alternative. Also, shrinking packages is a must. Those white strawberries are a neat novelty….but not for $5. Think of the retail price, and work *your way back. I think the days of 3lb bags being standard in potatoes and apples are over. Who can afford an $8 bag of apples?*

The Deli

In many ways, the **deli** and **foodservice** are related from the customer's perspective, and in many merchandising departments. For the purpose of a store walk, though, we're going to keep them separate. Probably the best way to think about it is the difference between **hot food** and **cold food**, with cold food being in the deli. The deli is the area selling things to be eventually put together and consumed at home or out somewhere. The one main ready to eat product in the deli are the **sandwiches**, and there is a decent argument that even sandwiches should be in the foodservice area. The best way to stay on trend is to think like a customer. Have we said that before? Maybe a few thousand times.

The deli is an area being pressured by the *health and wellness* trend, like every other category and department in the store. The health and wellness trend has forced another look at the amounts of nitrates, sodium, and additives that have been thrown into processed meats- then labeled as healthy. In some cases, eating a deli meat sandwich is just as bad for your body as a Big Mac with fries! Things are changing for the better, and we'll all be healthier for it.

There is a "processed and cured meats rejection" happening in this country. We're seeing products labeled as unprocessed, uncured, etc. The only issue is deli meat is a bit like jerky. It *needs* something to bind it and preserve it.

How do we win in the deli? After everything we've said about processed meats, **deli meats** and **cheeses** are still popular, as are the deli salads. One of the best practices in the deli involves a *three-tier pricing structure* and variety. Everything else revolves around these two principles.

For the three-tier pricing, it is commonly known amongst customers that you can flex in and out of the fat content of deli meats. It is also commonly known that the price will fluctuate with the quality levels. Some customers just want a **cheap product** they can feed their family. A rock solid price on ham, turkey, yellow American cheese, and maybe a roast beef is necessary to satisfy a certain segment of the population. If you do not offer that tier today, do not be afraid to attack it. In multiple retailers, it has been proven that an opening price point deli meat offer *does not cannibalize* the better quality cuts. It just brings people back over to the deli that had been skipping you and going to a price-only operator.

For the other tiers, you need a quality product that is **national brand equivalent** store brand- plus maybe a national brand (think Sara Lee). Then, you need a **quality tier** brand, like Boar's Head. You may choose to also offer a store brand in the higher quality tier, but be careful. That might become a major area of spoilage, if you are trying to sell a store brand next to Boar's Head or Dietz and Watson.

Then, take care of variety, like all the **Italian cuts**, the more obscure cuts, the varieties of cheeses, and anything that helps you shout assortment. These cuts do not need to be low priced, as that is not why people are buying them. Keep them wrapped until a customer wants them, and wrap immediately after. They do not have a ton of volume, so watch for shrink. Keep variety, though. Do not control yourself out of business.

What's the top trend in the deli? In-store made **guacamole and hummus**. The multiple ways we can incorporate guacamole and hummus into our diets is astounding, and *mostly healthy*. If you can sub hummus for mayo, that's a healthy alternative. **Red beet hummus** is rocking! Think from a customer viewpoint (there it is again!), we all know beets and avocados are healthy. *Well, how much* *fun is it to take a beet bunch and slice it and cook it?* It's a mess, you look like you're bleeding, and you have this massive green top that is supposed to be healthy, but tastes like sand and grit. **Solution: red beet hummus**.

Now the guac. Avocados are like these little cantankerous angry things that love to act like they will ripen nicely and evenly. But what happens? Yes, you go to bed and they are green and hard, the next morning they are brown and ready to be thrown away! **Solution: guacamole**. The customers usually invent solutions before the food industry does. That's why we stress "customer first" at all times.

A few other points on the deli. *Face the slicers towards the customers.* It's a simple thing, but makes a huge difference in appearance and implied customer service. The associate takes the order, grabs the wrapped meat, and takes it around the table to then face the customer while cutting. Seems small, but it isn't. The rule for anything in a store is to avoid turning your back to the customer.

Last thing on deli (we'll get to cheese and pizza later) is *scheduling*. Watch your labor in the deli during peak shopping periods. Cutting labor in the deli is a self-fulfilling prophecy. You keep cutting, the *sales go down* accordingly. Cut some more, and *sales go down again*. When sales go down, you then cut labor. Stop it! Some customers will wait in line for their chance at the deli slicing associate, but some won't. Those are the silent voters who looked at the line, and decided it wasn't worth their time or effort. In other words, you have no idea how much you can sell because you are eliminating those who *do not want to wait*. They'll go somewhere else.

Are there things you can do to help alleviate the pressure when busy? Of course. **Pre-slice** the high volume meats. Pre-slice the ham, turkey, American cheese, roast beef, and maybe even bologna or whatever is on sale that week. I've never seen a customer balk at it. You can also **pre-package** deli salads, and have a spot on the floor for anyone who does not want to wait. Excellent solution.

Speaking of deli salads, you really just need to focus on **macaroni salad and potato salad**. These two are the big kids on the block. You need variety, but these two salads are more than 50% of your deli salad sales (including red skin potato salad). The deli is a quality and signature area for many retailers, and needs to be run by someone with a keen view on how to maximize sales while controlling shrink. *Control, don't eliminate.* Eliminate shrink and you'll eliminate your sales. Have plenty of areas with sandwich breads, toppings, etc. and you can complete a picnic right there in the department.

One other thing to consider is **fresh pasta**. Walmart moved all fresh pasta products into the deli. Many other retailers keep those products adjacent to the deli. Whatever you do, shelving these items, along with homemade pizza-making supplies, hummus, cheeses, etc., makes for a robust presentation of these types of items. I say "these types", because they really do not have an inherent home or category. They need refrigeration, are seen as toppings (like hummus and spreads), go well with charcuterie trays (all the rage right now), and present themselves well near the specialty cheese sections.

Inflation Tips: Besides finding less quality meats and cheeses to offer affordable prices, going with smaller containers and serving sizes is obligatory in this department. The consumer still wants product, but cannot afford as much as in the past. Give them serving sizes that are affordable and still satisfy their need to feed their family.

The Ready to Eat

The reason I separated foodservice from the deli is the incredible growth that is coming from the **foodservice** side of the business. In today's world of grocerants- a hybrid of grocery store and restaurant, the old days of potato logs and fried chicken are over. Add **ghost kitchens**, or areas in the kitchen designated solely for takeout and delivery, plus inflation, and this part of the business is rocking!

First thing's first, *hire someone with restaurant experience* for this area of your store. You are proactively offering a dining out or dining at-home option to your customers. You are working with, or competing against, restaurants and real chefs. You need restaurant expertise. Now, having said that, make sure it is a restaurateur (yes, that is the correct spelling) who either understands grocery stores, or can learn quickly.

And, where do you go from here? The sky's the limit. With the right amount of imagination, combined with the appropriate demographic customer, this area of your store can be the area everyone talks about! First, though, you can stop reading if you just do this: *Copy everything Wegmans is doing and bring in enough volume to support the operation profitably.* Do that, and you're fine. Stop reading.

All kidding aside, Wegmans does an outstanding job in their restaurants. But, you may want to make sure you have enough customer traffic to offer what they do. Otherwise, just doing what they do is going to be the death knell to profitability. For everyone else, let's talk about how to put the offer together.

Let's talk about **cold** and **hot** differences first. The ability to offer a large assortment of **cold prepared foods** is desirable. Cold pizzas, cold chicken, cold everything, they are all fine and part of a convenient offer. But do not confuse offering cold food to be heated at home as running a restaurant. It is necessary for your assortment offer, but does not differentiate you. *The hot foods are your differentiator.*

The most visible highest volume item of them all? The **rotisserie chicken**, or the roaster! The largest tonnage item in most prepared foods areas tends to be the rotisserie chicken. It was first on the block, it was highly touted as one of the first meal solutions offered by grocery stores, and it still reigns supreme today. As with everything else in this book, you still need to pay attention to health and wellness. These things can be sodium-packed! At some point, work on your offer to the degree where you can reduce the sodium content without impacting taste.

You can address trends by ensuring you carry **organic rotisserie chickens**, and make sure you communicate they are *probiotic free, pesticide free, growth hormone free*, etc. They will cost more, so the customer wants to know why. If you're looking for a "secret recipe", try to break down the Costco rotisserie program and seasonings. It's a great chicken and is not loaded with sodium. Every customer knows the rotisserie chicken is a signature item at Costco, and probably the most affordable way to feed your family day in and day out.

For the flavors, *regular is the top seller*, then please make sure you have a variety of flavors. Most customers will pick up a regular *and* a flavored bird. That's how customers think- I'll choose a "safe" one and then spread my wings (couldn't help it) and try a new flavor. Make sure you have a steady supply of roasters cooking throughout the day and can meet demand for the afternoon shopper. Do not cook everything in the morning and let it sit there all day. Once you have established a solid business of rotisserie chickens, try some rotisserie turkey breasts, etc. They all sell well.

Environmental scanning tip: get into the club stores and see what they are doing for roasters, as well as everything else. Club stores love the rotisserie chicken statement, like we just said about Costco. They tend to have a bigger bird (cooked weight around 36 ounces) and a better price. Compare to the traditional grocery store's 26-28 ounce cooked weight, and you can see the issue.

One of the most difficult aspects of grocery store foodservice is being able to be *trendy*. It takes a long time for new techniques and new preparation methods to make their way into the operation. But, being trendy is how you stay relevant. When sushi was on an uptrend, most stores found someone who knew what they were doing and offered them a space to sell their goods. Similarly, find some chefs or cooks and work with them as a test kitchen for new offers and new items.

Name one grocery store in the country that joined the chicken sandwich debate between Popeye's and Chick fil A. Burritos, acai bowls, chicken and waffles, and just keep going. Trend is difficult in foodservice, but necessary.

Now, what about **pizza**? Great opportunity to have another differentiator in the hot foods area. In many ways, the grocery store can offer a *better selection* of pizza, have more affordable lunch options, and take care of customers *better* than pizzerias that are covering all their overhead expenses with one commodity. The only issue....the pizzerias deliver. If you really want to establish yourself in the pizza business, figure out a way to **deliver the pizza**. And do it like the pizza shops- *piping hot, friendly drivers*, etc. And, make sure you have **Detroit style pizza**! It is a super-hot trend, and it seems like only the delivery pizza places are reacting to it.

The rest of the foods to be offered hot? That would be

driven primarily by the demographics surrounding the store. **Asian food, Mexican food, soups, a service hot bar**. They all can work, if you know your potential for lunch, your potential for dinner, the customers surrounding your store, etc. A word of caution, if you want to establish yourself as a place for dinner, be open and ready for dinner *during dinner time*. That is one of the quickest ways to drive people to "real" restaurants that are open late. Remember, grocery stores are not known as places to visit late for anything fresh. We can change that perception.

Let's talk **sushi** one more time. Although sometimes served hot in restaurants, it's customarily a cold offer in grocery stores, and most customers look in the foodservice area for sushi. Not only is sushi a high dollar sale at the register, but nobody buys just one pack! Treat sushi like a *signature area* of the store! An authentic sushi offer is table stakes these days. Have a regular assortment, have a cooked section and raw, then try new limited time only offers-like flaming hot Cheeto's sushi. Sushi can be a super area of the store to show you know food!

This area of the store has *so much potential* for trend, for awareness, for repeat traffic, for takeout, for drive-through....just keep going. It's a fun part of the store!

Inflation Tips: It's all about the hot bar! The roaster chicken can be supplemented with a full turkey breast cooked, 8-piece chicken dinners, chicken sandwiches, etc. When inflationary times hit, going out to eat is rejected in favor of eating at home. You can even have point of sale material touting the price per family member. This is truly a place customers can fight inflation!

The Bakery

As we make our way from foodservice, we have this big, bountiful, beautiful **bakery** department! And, yes, it should look just like that. There is no excuse to have an anêmic looking bakery offer. Not everything in the department is incredibly healthy for you, but it *sure does taste good*. Plus, bread has this connection to the earth that is unmistakable.

The best way to ensure the bakery department has an excellent appearance and suitable variety, is to divide into segments consisting of **"carriers"** (yes, bread is a carrier of everything) and **sweets**. Once you look at it that way, you can then go about allocating space in your "carrier" section for **artisanal breads** traditionally used to "carry" a topping, like baguettes, French bread, and most crusty breads. Great for olive oil, butter, hummus, and those kinds of toppings.

That's not the only use for those breads, just the primary use, you then need a selection of the same types of **breads sliced**- especially sourdough, pumpernickel, and those normally used for sandwiches. Having the bakery so close to the deli makes perfect tie-in opportunities. Rolls and other packaged buns can also be in this section. As a rule, make sure those ugly white pricing labels with all the ingredients listed are facing down. The star of the show is the bread, not the label. But, please make sure the labels are correctly completed, so those who have celiac (or those just avoiding gluten) can find what they want in the bakery.

A money making idea? Take half your batch of **French bread** and add **garlic spread** to it, then place it in those foil packs you can place directly in the oven (make sure it is actually the one you can place in the oven without a fire).

A germ prevention idea? In the "old days", artisanal breads were open at the top, so they could cool. As you might imagine, today's packaging will need to be *entirely enclosed* all the way around the product. As much as we love the idea of handing someone a loaf of bread, make sure all cleanliness guidelines are in place.

What about **locally baked bread**? This is somewhere you'll need to make a decision. Do you fight local bakeries and carry your own, or embrace local and bring everyone up together? I'd vote for teamwork. Local artisan bread will never take all your business, and it shows you are connected to your community. *Carry the local breads, and your customers will appreciate it.*

On to the **sweet stuff**! The bountiful abundance of products doesn't stop with the "carriers". The sweet goods are just as important, if not *more* important. More important as sweet goods are usually *unplanned impulse* purchases. Walking around seeing baked products is similar to why customers walk around farmer's markets. Almost every purchase is incremental, and is great for the retailer (and the person consuming it). Sweet goods should scream "buy me!".

Start with those handheld bundles of joy! **Cookies**! Perfect for snacking, after school, really anytime. **Chocolate chip** leads the way, as Captain Obvi would state. *If you're out of chocolate chip, you're out of cookies.* Big buckets, large cookies, small cookies, decadent, over the top....you cannot have enough chocolate chip cookies. Their little forgotten siblings oatmeal raisin, sugar, peanut butter, or macadamias are to be carried; but, only if you took care of the OG CC first. And, by the way, the club stores are all over cookies (and cakes and pies and all sweet goods). If you want to be in the cookie business, you need to have an idea of how the club stores view cookies, especially around the holidays.

As for **cakes**, you should have a full lineup of *sheet*

cakes and special occasion cakes, along with *cupcakes* of the same flavors, even the smaller "cake pieces" sold as "for one"- not a cupcake and not a cake, a piece of cake. As for flavors, definitely *chocolate and vanilla* base layers, then go crazy from there with types of frosting. Keep in mind, **sheet cakes** are usually for special occasions. The variety **artisan cakes** are the "try me" cakes, like German chocolate, strawberry, devil's food, and my all-time favorite: carrot cake (with cream cheese frosting and little raisins).

Your cake decorator should be as passionate about cakes as your floral person is about the floral department. This is the one part of the store where you can truly tell who has passion and who is just "dialing it in". Passion wins every time!

And, how about **doughnuts and bagels**? Absolutely! Primarily morning-focused, you need a variety of glazed and jelly-filled doughnuts, as well as the "everything" bagel, blueberry, and plain. Have the variety, and encourage the customers to buy in bulk. This department can still stand out as a playland for *decadence and taste*!

Inflation Tips: As with everything, you may need to shrink the size of all your goods, just to ensure a customer sees an attractive price point. And, you know, it might just help with their diets. A smaller bagel, smaller doughnut, small pieces of cake, bread and rolls that weigh less, etc. should all be on your assortment list. That's the direction you'll need to go to remain affordable, especially when the items are impulsive, like bakery bread and sweet goods. The first products cut back in inflationary times will always be the ones that are not necessarily on anyone's shopping list.

The Seafood

Talk about a department where the tide has been rising the last few years, in alignment with the trend towards health and wellness, the **seafood** department is poised to continue that trend, *if….if*, we can *keep the impact of inflation from polluting the waters.* We may have a new generation of vegetarians on the way, and it would have everything to do with the *price of proteins*. When you start to see **red snapper** and **sockeye salmon** hovering around $15/lb. or more, the more viable alternative is to doctor up some *pasta*. Pasta has gone up in price, too, but not like all the proteins- fish included.

Inflation is a big story, but let's put it aside for a minute and focus on the department. Let's talk about how the set looks. Any store selling *food* has a need for a *seafood* department. If you are in a lower income area, or are a price-oriented store, then it might be best to go with wrapped fresh or frozen seafood. And, if you're heading in that direction, then the types of seafood are more towards bulk than specialized. A Pacific halibut does not belong in these stores. **Flounder, shrimp, haddock, surimi, tilapia, farmed salmon** are the types of fish that are affordable and able to be offered at competitive price points for those who are mostly looking for something relatively healthy to feed their families.

And, speaking of feeding your family affordably, make sure you have multiple forms of seafood to offer as well: the **fully unadulterated** fish, the **uncooked but seasoned** fish, and the **cooked** fish. Not everyone knows what to do with seafood. And, in the cooked section, make sure you have an ample selection of **fried seafood**, mostly haddock and shrimp. Since it is served cold, it's also able to be purchased on SNAP, and you should point this out as a convenience to those customers using SNAP. And, in a recession, those on SNAP benefits will continue to increase. *Cold fried is a super area to drive incremental volume in seafood!*

In some retailers, they will offer to *fry anything* for anyone. Anything in the case can be chosen and fried right there in the seafood department. It works well, and gives the customer the sense of being in a downhome fish fry. Make sure you have some kind of hush puppies or french fries, along with some cole slaw. Served as a dinner, and talked up as Fish Frydays (or something corny like that), and you may find yourself selling around 10% of your seafood volume as fried fish! And, once again, you make more gross profit, offer a unique experience to your guests, and may offer something other competitors do not.

Now, let's talk about the *higher-end stores*, where the demand for seafood is significant. Everyone knows seafood is good for you, but not all can afford it. Those who *can* afford it, *usually buy it*. In these stores, you should be offering a *service seafood case*, where you train your seafood professionals to talk about recipes, how to best prepare, how to best serve, what's new, all the things someone would appreciate as they are planning how to feed their family. *A well-trained fishmonger is essential in higher demographic stores.*

In these stores, quite important, steer away from farm-raised, unless it's something like **trout**- which is usually sustainably farmed. The media on farm-raised has been so bad, there's a good chance the industry will never convince anyone that a farm-raised fish is good for them. *Wild caught* is the preferred fish for anyone who can afford it, and filling your case with farm-raised will mostly raise the suspicion that you have no idea what you are doing.

Remember, customers are trusting *you* to maintain the

cold chain, maintain the cleanliness of your cases (*if you can smell the seafood, don't buy any from that store*), source your fish sustainably and socially consciously....it's a big responsibility.

You need to accept that customers are looking for a base variety (**primarily sockeye salmon, haddock, cod, perch, trout**, etc.) and then a mix of in and out items like **halibut, red snapper**, etc. Read up on trends and healthy items, and feature those kinds of items. A customer in this kind of store is up to date on health trends in every department. Ensure there is a good mix of lake fish and ocean fish, and communicate with the customers the importance of cooking certain varieties more than others (lake fish needs to be cooked longer).

And, keep in mind allergies, like shellfish allergies. **Maintaining a barrier between shellfish and fin fish is a must**, as is changing your gloves between orders if a fin fish and shell fish is ordered. This allergy is deadly, so do not take it lightly. In fact, it might be best to have little tin trays for each type of fish. The least amount of liquid mixing between species, the better off the customers (and the stores) will be.

How about **lobsters or octopus**? There are certain species of fish or crustaceans that are showing a tendency to "think" or "react". You have to make up your own mind on this one. There's a reason we don't carry dolphin in our stores (or dogs or rabbits, or any other animals sometimes domesticated). Like I said, make a decision as a company and stick with it. If you happen to be in a predominantly Asian market (where **live fish** is customary), and have no idea how Asians eat seafood, you might want to get up to speed quickly. Either buy the expertise (acquire someone), or hire an expert. You need to understand the Asian customs, preferences, normal selections, and how the Asian customers like to choose their fish (usually live and swimming).

And you cannot talk seafood without talking **shrimp**! Shrimp are a go-to item for parties, get-togethers, holidays, super recipes, etc. Have multiple types of shrimp in the fresh case, as well as the frozen case. *Cooked and uncooked, peeled and unpeeled*, and even the surimi rings posing as shrimp rings.

Another area where you can show a ton of variety, but not have it spoil so quickly, for you or for the customer, is in the **frozen seafood** section. Not frozen fish like fish sticks, frozen seafood like **wild caught red snapper, coho salmon, branzino, sea bass, tuna, swordfish, and halibut**. Use the frozen section to expand variety, while not worrying as much about the fish going bad in two days.

Inflation Tips: This is going to be a tough department in an inflationary time. The best thing going for fish is the fact that turkey, beef, chicken, and pork are all rushing to be the same price as fish! It's all going up, and it's going to fundamentally change the way customers shop for the proteins to feed their families.   The best bet is to continue offering smaller packages, and finding fish varieties that may be much less expensive- like tilapia.

The Meat

The **meat** department is a signature area for any store. You must have a quality offering, large variety, affordable packs, and excitement. It's a lot to ask of a department, but well worth it. Similar to meat's blue friend the fish, *inflation is having a major impact on the meat department*. Luckily (?), the meat department has been through this before. If handled properly, a meat department can operate quite well in an inflationary time.

We'll lead the meat discussion with the top tip for an inflationary time, or a recession: **train the meat cutters to package the product with the <u>end price point</u> in mind.** It's the most impactful thing you can do to help the customers during these times! In the past, you lowered the price per pound, and then made the packs as large as possible. You needed volume. Today, with the price per pound so much higher, even a discounted product is going to be inordinately expensive when packaged in a larger "family size" or "value pack". Give explicit instructions to ensure there are packages of red meat under $10, between $10-$15, and then $15 and up.

Know who caught on to this issue first? Walmart. They started calling everything **thin sliced**. There would still be four or five pieces of whatever the cut of meat was, but they were thinner now. In essence, the package still looked like you could feed your family, and it also looked affordable. They made this change in both red meat, as well as pork products. Nice job by Walmart on that one.

Next, make sure you have plenty of **grass fed, organic, No-No-No** red meat (meaning no preservatives, no antibiotics, no anything added). There is a future for grass

57

fed, and that may be the brightest future for red meat. "Regular" red meat, full of preservatives, high yield feed, tight cages, and unhealthy animals will still sell, but the heyday is over. Most people who avoided meat because it upset their stomachs have figured out *grass-fed* alleviates the digestion part of the meat experience.

The **plant-based** option came on strong, and has now settled. As a food retailer, it's important to offer the options for the customers, and let them make up their own minds. I'd suggest you stay away from the word "alternative" in all categories. If people want to avoid certain meats or cuts or animals, that is solely up to their discretion- it's an *option*. You're a food store, and you offer options. After a euphoric rise in trend, mainly because there were so few plant-based products previously, these products leveled off for a while and now have a more steady runway in front of them. To the degree plant-based might be cheaper to make, I'd expect steadily increasing growth for the foreseeable future.

Pay attention to **grilling steaks** in the summer, **roasts** in the winter. Maybe have a *Summer in January* sale, just to try something new. You'd be surprised how many people will buy a steak just because you made it interesting. *Local ranchers* and focusing on *knowing where the beef has come from*, is trending. Knowing the source of all our foods is something desired by customers, and we're here to help. And while doing so, it's also a great practice for merchants of food to understand the entire supply chain.

One more point on red meat *packaging*. There is a groundswell of acceptance of what we call **vac packs** of red meat being available to the customer. We could call it the "Wegmans effect". For years, Wegmans has been one of the few chains to offer red meat in a vacuum-sealed packs to the customers. The benefits of this pack to the consumer are enormous. This type of packaging offers excellent dating, gives more time to use the product before having to freeze it, is ready when you need it (not having to be thawed), and is all-around one of the most consumer-friendly packs available. Definitely something to consider, when thinking customer-first.

Let's move on to **pork**. Another category that is seeing inflationary pressures. Make sure you have *organics or natural*, have some thick cut and some thin cut, have some large trays and some small trays, and stay in stock. The pork industry tried the "Pork....the other white meat" campaign", and it was able to get pork on the radar for a little while. Now, it's a solid category that should have a wide assortment of various sizes.

One area with a nice trend is the previously mentioned vac packs when applied to pork. In fact, we're seeing quite a number of new items in vac pack in pork. Thinking customer-first, most consumers worry about drying out their pork when cooked. **Seasoned packs of pork** help solve that issue for customers. Seasoned pork tenderloins can be stored for multiple days, are pre-seasoned, can be cut into any size the customer wants, etc.

Chicken! What was once described as the healthy alternative to red meat, chicken is now under a major attack for well....the fact we now seem to be growing "super chickens". The feed given to chickens these days is turning them into monsters! Other than that, chicken seems to be the category discussed the most when inflation is mentioned. There were some strong crosscurrents of production plant issues, supply issues, and then we had the *Great Chicken Sandwich Wars*! As one person stated, **chickens only have two breasts**....when Popeye's, McDonald's, and Chick Fil A decide to battle each other with chicken breast sandwiches, *it puts quite a strain on supply.*

Same tactics apply with chicken, as they have with

fish, beef, pork, all proteins. Place smaller portions in packages, show a family of four they can still offer some meat on each plate, spread out on organic, natural, no preservatives, no antibiotics, etc. The "truth in labeling" for chickens is going to be the issue for poultry in the future. The sections of "smart chicken", and "free of everything bad chicken" continue to expand.

What about the rest? You have **hams**, which tend to peak either around Christmas and Easter, and then the next most popular times are related to being cold out and maybe hosting many guests- like Super Bowl. **Turkeys**, just one time a year. That's it. You know, turkeys for .19/lb. or even .49/lb. are the best protein deal in the store. The amount of time to prep a turkey is the reason they haven't caught on for occasions other than Thanksgiving, but they are a great value.

Where can you make a difference in sales and margin in the meat department? Frozen is a solid growth area. Think specialty **frozen burgers, appetizers, meal kits, chicken breasts**, etc. Good growth areas. Another way? Meat bundles. I love meat bundles! Where you have the clientele receiving money once or twice a month from the government, bundling meat packs into $50 bundles, $75 bundles, and even $150 bundles can sell a ton of meat to people who feel the need to stock up for a month. A pack focused on affordable meats to feed your family for two weeks to a month is a great way to help families in inflationary periods.

And **service meat cases**, where a customer can speak to a meat associate and pick out his or her own meat cuts? Yes, there is still a place for service meat counters. That is a high demographic, though. Most customers assume the service meat case products are better quality and more expensive. On one hand (price), they are correct. On the other (quality), they had better be correct. Make it known the service meat case is not for re-conditioning product that did not sell in the self-serve case.

One other area, **meat grinds**. Make sure the quality control and integrity are maintained in the process. Labeling something 80/20 ground beef, and it's not- that's a bad idea. Customers are quite tuned in to meat fat content, chuck, sirloin, etc. Plus, the government would like you to sell what you say you are selling.

Lunch meat, **bacon, sausages, hot dogs, bratwurst** and the perimeter areas of the meat department have grown in importance. For one (and not a great reason), they are highly preserved, so last a while at home. And second, they're mostly affordable. If you're looking to feed your kids, a hot dog or some bologna is just right. Unfortunately, though, *there is a still a major price gap between the healthier packs and the unhealthier packs*. Closing that gap could shift customers into a better for them product.

Meat is an integral reason customers shop stores, and should be thought of as an *identity department*. Fresh, well-culled, well-rotated, full assortment, full seasonal offering, it's part of the reason people will choose your store. When you do this, you meat their demands everyday.

Inflation Tips: Consistent with the seafood department, smaller packs are the best way to help a family still offer a meat protein on each plate. It might have been 8oz. in the past and is now 4oz., but four 4oz. cuts of meat can still be surrounded by leafy greens and vegetables and/or pasta. Customers are doing everything to stretch their money, and we can help.

The Refrigerated

Let's talk **dairy** and refrigerated. What a cool department in which to differentiate your store! Please do not just call it a **dairy** anymore. How's that for step one? There are *so many* people looking for dairy options, just call it the **refrigerated section**- because that's what it is. Let's go through a few sections and see what we can find.

Start with **yogurt**. Probably the hottest ~~dairy~~ refrigerated category in the last few years. The health benefits are enormous, and most people are recognizing the value of the *positive bacteria* in your gut (see kombucha), and yogurt tastes great (don't see kombucha). The same benefits are also seen in **cottage cheese**, where fruit-added cottage cheese is trying to make its presence known.

Then, there's **Greek yogurt**. Started by a non-Greek company in Upstate New York (Chobani), Greek is about as Greek as a pickle. But, it *does* have extra protein, *does* provide health benefits, and there *are* some packages that try to limit the sugar. All in all, the benefits outweigh the sugar.

With growth comes competition, so along comes Icelandic **skyr**. Skyr describes the process which makes the product *even thicker* and *even better* for you. It's skyr, not yogurt. A slew of skyrs have seen success! Add additional methods of producing a cultured dairy cheese or milk product, like Australian yogurt, etc., and you have a growth category.

The category is a force to be reckoned with. One area to watch, which we've discussed in most categories, is *plant-based*. Technically, **almond, soy, hemp**, and the other dairy alternatives are plant-based; so, they will continue to grow in all areas of the store, mostly dairy and meat.

Then you have **kefir**, **drinkable yogurts**, anything

fermented, etc., to round out a smokin' hot category. Everything is being turned into drinkable form, plus a distinction between adults and children is also becoming prevalent in this section. Strangely enough, organic and grass fed are not as highly accentuated in this section. They are available, but are not the drivers of consumption. The drivers of the consumer decision tree are sugar and protein content.

Next in line with growth, happened around the same time, is the explosion of **milk options**. Soy milk (*beverage*, it's not really milk) used to be fringy, but now soy is front and center, and joined by hemp and almond and a whole bunch of ways to make something *taste like milk without being milk*. The poor little cow has been squeezed out to about 50% of the category it invented. It's not your job to singlehandedly save the dairy farmers. Watch for the **pistachio milk** trend in this section. The customers vote, and you want to win their vote. One thing to keep in mind, both in the stores and at home- ***"Don't give milk a warm welcome!"***- get it into the refrigerator as it comes off the truck!

Cheese is next in line. Cheese in the refrigerated section is stable. There are only just so many new flavors you can produce. Where cheese has *taken off* is in the <u>deli</u> section. We grocers need to come to a conclusion as to how not to have cheese in multiple locations. The best way to get a customer to trade up is to put the unique items next to the top sellers. At this point, the *unique items* are handled by the deli, while the *top sellers* are handled by the dairy department. But, having said that, the hottest segment in cheese follows the trend everywhere else, look for healthier products like grass-fed, organic.

Eggs, the best growth in eggs is….say it with me….yup, *organic, cage free, healthy, omega added*, etc. If you get anything out of this book, it's that we are becoming a healthy world. It's a great trend, and we should embrace it. A growth area in eggs? **Hard boiled and peeled eggs.** Once again, customer-first focus. Customers love hard boiled eggs! They are convenient and you can just pop 'em in your mouth, cut them up in salads, add them to your ramen, etc. They are difficult to boil and peel correctly. Such a simple, but highly frustrating, process. Then someone comes along with boiled and peeled. Magic! Watch these things. They are hot!

The rest of the refrigerated section has been stable. **Butter** is trying to be healthy, with grass fed, real butter, taking the yellow coloring out, etc. Kerrygold has a super following, and is one of the true grass fed butters. **Cookie dough** was hot for a while (but eaten cold), went through a bit of an issue with bacteria, and now there's a whole line of "edible cold" cookie dough. Many retailers shelve the **refrigerated bagels** in the refrigerated section, near **cream cheese**. This makes a ton of sense to customers. Shows you are focused on them, and solves the issue of where to put the bagels.

One of the worst trending major sections in the refrigerated case would be **orange juice**. Poor OJ ☹ Had a great run, with an aura of healthiness, until somebody analyzed it and found a pile of sugar, found that processing fruits takes most of the goodness out of them, found that companies were taking sub-par juice from Chile and mixing it with a little Florida, etc. *This section will continue to shrink over time*, just like the shelf-stable juice section. It's a sign of the times.

There is a growth trend in this area around mixed lemonades, anything Newman's Own, pomegranate juice, and anything related to superberries. If you read the ingredients, you could have the same issue as with orange juice, but it doesn't seem to made the connection with the customer. One hypothesis, though, is these mixes are trending up in parallel with the trend in **vodka**. Unless you're "pre-gaming" shots, a drink like Tito's is darn tasty with some type of fruit and sugar drink.

One of the hottest trends in the refrigerated section is making a **breakfast section**, consisting of **ready to eat breakfast packs** (there are eight feet sections in some stores!), **refrigerated bagels and biscuits, microwave hash browns and shredded potatoes**, etc. What a neat and....customer-first section! Watch this section, as ready to eat packs are showing up all over the store. Included in this area would be **canned RTD coffee**. It's showing up in almost all refrigerated sections, and deserves a seat at the table.

The refrigerated category is an interesting one, and demands the need to flex in and out of categories as they trend up and down. One way to add flexibility is to make a **cheese section** in a *separate area of your store*. Combining the cheese you'd normally find in the refrigerated section with the cheese you find in the deli section, and the cheese you find in the meat department, may come across as a robust and bountiful "cheese world", and allow you to cut some cheese redundancies at the same time.

Inflation Tips: I'm going to sound like a broken record, but smaller packs are the rule of the land. And as we're working our way into center store, a robust store brand program will help win over shoppers. Store brands have always dominated the egg section, but not as much in the juices or even kefir. Expanding your store brand offer is paramount to helping customers navigate inflation.

The Frozen

Let's talk about **frozen**. Almost everything in the freezer is a replication of something you can find elsewhere in the store, so the frozen section reflects the same trends as the rest of the store. What holds true for *shelf-stable* desserts, holds true for *frozen* desserts. What holds true for *shelf-stable* juice, holds true for *frozen* juice. You get it.

What we will talk about is the amazingly positive trend frozen is having right now! As shoppers are considering how to feed their family with wholesome foods, throw away less spoiled foods, and offer a variety of dishes that make life exciting, *frozen foods are right there with them*!

Let's talk about the two major categories that are the most popular in the frozen food section: **pizza and ice cream**! Yeah! Say pizza and ice cream, and you've got a party! Let's talk about pizza first. Pizza has been, and remains, an all-around everlastingly popular food, snack, breakfast, hangover remedy. You name it. **Pizza rocks!**

On this one, the big challenge is to make sure customers buy enough to *always have some on hand*. If they don't have it on hand when the pizza monster rears its big purple head? Yup, they order it from that big bad delivery spot that takes $3 worth of ingredients, cooks it for you in eight minutes, and charges you $12, with a service charge, delivery charge, and driver tip! Or, they make it a little bigger, pair it with a Coke and some wings, and ding you for $50. And why do we do it? *Because everyone loves the pizza person!*

Make sure you constantly have stock-up sales on pizza, so it's there when the customers want it. Plus, you know what I'm going to say....make sure you are in business on the healthy brands or versions, like **Amy's Organic**

Pizzas, Newman's Own, thin-sliced, clean ingredients, etc. It's a trend. You're not trying to alienate places like Domino's, but a frozen pizza is the ultimate fun food for all occasions. I cannot see where pizza will ever die in popularity. Just not going to happen. *Not as long as I'm around!*

What about **ice cream**? We offer every form and flavor of ice cream possible, and volume keeps growing! Sure, we might look at healthier versions once in a while, but you don't eat ice cream as a health food. *It's indulgent, it's fun, it's a kid favorite, it's an adult favorite!*

Big buckets of ice cream for parties, little containers for when you break up, moshi for "high end" nights, regular containers for after dinner, novelties to have around during the summer, it's all there. Everyone knows ice cream is mostly unhealthy and they don't care. If you want to be healthy, don't eat it. But, it's good stuff. YOLO! One thing to keep in mind- ***"If you're out of vanilla, you're out of ice cream!"*-** keep vanilla in stock. Make sure vanilla has plenty of room!

The other trends in frozen food? The **frozen berry** section took off at the same time as the slushie blender craze took off, so that was a bump in sales. For the most part, frozen berries still maintain their healthy goodness and are an excellent healthy choice, and sales are even. Just don't add sugar or yogurt or something. Add bananas. Nature's perfect snack. Good section, but we've seen some leveling in demand here.

Appetizers, sure they have a nice niche around the holidays, but most people see them as a salt-laden junk food. Well, except **pizza rolls**....pizza rolls! The popularity of pizza pervades over into appetizers. Anything handheld and pizza-related is popular. Pizza rolls will live forever!

Frozen vegetables are on a tear! First, have you ever tried to push a peapod out of a fresh pea? Yeah, it kind of sucks as an activity, and *peas are so good for you*! Enter the frozen pea! Now, translate that scenario to broccoli, corn, etc. and you can see why frozen vegetables are having a fun time! Make sure you have a mix of "cook in bag" and larger bags that are apportioned as you are cooking. They both have a place in the customer's freezer.

The rest of the sections that could make up a meal, including **fish sticks, fish fillets, frozen breaded chicken, pierogies, frozen waffles and biscuits, plant-based frozen products**, etc.? Remember, the trends in *non-frozen* reflect the trends in *frozen*. Salty frozen chicken is now being replaced by *natural, antibiotic free*, chicken. Egg biscuits are now partnering with plant-based biscuits. It's all there, and it's all customer-focused!

Let's talk **de-sku'ing** of healthy lines. Not getting rid of them, but de-sku'ing. Certainly the brands will tell you differently, but the customers have their own way of choosing switchability versus walkability (if you're out of an item, will you switch or walk (leave)). We have entire aisles of quite similar healthy brands, and there is always pressure on assortment in frozen. This is the area I'd look to first.

Inflation Tips: Besides the aforementioned smaller packs and sizes, one key area in frozen is showing how you waste so much less food when you buy frozen, <u>and</u> add variety to your life at the same time. Buying a fresh fish fillet or fresh berries means you have started your countdown clock towards spoiling. You don't use it, it goes in the trash or compost. For frozen, that problem is solved for you. The more we can get the message out about the sustainability of frozen foods, the more we can help the customers.

The Alcohol

For the next three sections, we're going to talk **alcohol**. I'm giving each of the "traditional" sections their own spot; but, if you're in this business, you know *it's all merging in the eyes of the consumer*. The most interesting part of the store right now is watching what's going on with alcohol.

This book is sold all over the country, so I have to note many of you *cannot sell* **all three types of alcohol** in your stores. We have federal, state, and county laws in the United States about only being able to choose one alcohol (usually beer), being able to sell two (beer and wine), all three (beer, wine, sprits), beer and wine (but only wine under 14% abv (yes, it's a law), being able to sell it all 24 hours of every day, being able to sell it on every day except Sunday, being able to sell it only after noon on Sunday, etc. Being an alcohol buyer for a retailer is a testament to how many rules you can memorize about all your operating areas.

Then, you have the mandated three-tier distribution system, and cannot sell directly. Or can you? Sometimes you can go to a retailer, sometimes you can't. *Let's talk about some of the trends going on in alcohol.*

Blending of barriers. The first trend is the blurring of the three "types", for the consumer. What were previously clear and distinct differences between the types of alcohol have been blurred to an almost discernible point. Is it a **hard seltzer** or a **wine spritzer**? Is it a ready to drink **Moscow Mule** or a **Mule flavored malt beverage**? Why is the 4-pack of **Ketel One** cans $11.99 and the 12-pack of **High Noon** also $11.99? We're confusing the heck out of consumers! But, to defend the industry, *everyone is in everyone's shorts*; so, what are you supposed to do? You can't sit there and let someone take your business!

The best thing about the blending of the barriers is **everyone is trying everything**. The *trial and experiment* feel that was brought on by craft beer is now all over the alcohol section! It's a great time to be in alcohol, for both consumers and for the companies diversified enough to operate in all areas of alcohol.

Flavor is a barrier breaker. When you add flavors to traditionally unflavored items, it makes them more accessible. That's not such a bad thing, unless you only operate in one arena. Alcohol is expandable consumable, so you're always looking to make one more sale.

Trial is everywhere. As I just mentioned, everyone is trying everything. Especially in spirits, where mixing a drink might have been difficult to master, or maybe you didn't want 750ml of that spirit sitting around for months; or, you wanted to go on a boat and not bring a massive bottle of **Deep Eddy**. Flavors have made everything approachable.

It's a **double-edged sword**. Trial and lower *barriers to trial* also translate into difficult to obtain brand loyalty. It's fun, right? Put odd combinations and mixes out there and they keep selling. Then, as soon as you ramp up production, the customers *move on and try something else*. The term used lately to describe customer behavior in alcohol has been **brand promiscuity**. They move around and are loyal to very few brands.

What about the **non-alcohol trend**? Well, I don't know. Mocktails are cool, and NA items are necessary, but I wouldn't jump headfirst into this trend. Carry it, acknowledge it, and move on. Alcohol without alcohol is juice.

Keep these over-arching themes in mind as we head into discussing beer, wine, and spirits.

Inflation Tips: *Where proteins and produce and other items in the store are impacted by inflation, alcohol is a bit protected. Just keep prices within reason and we'll keep buying! Alcohol is a reward item for consumers, so it isn't nearly as sensitive. Are you really going to let a few bucks stand in the way of alcohol? Somehow, Ballast Point was able to charge $16.99 for a 6-pack of beer, and we bought it.*

The Beer

Still one of the hottest sections in the store is the **beer** section. And every year, another entrant into this crowded section makes it even more crowded. The people have spoken.

They want *variety*.

They want *treasure hunt*.

They practice *brand promiscuity*.

They want *healthy*.

They want *taste*.

They want convenience of *cans*.

They want taste of *bottles*.

They want *pre-mixed* spirits and soda.

They want *everything* from this section!

You can stop calling it the beer section. Seltzers and spritzers and ready to drink spirits have blurred the lines. Call it the **refrigerated alcohol** section. The switchability is high here. *If you're out of what I want, I'll just try something else.* As you can imagine, being in-stock is a *really big deal*. Planogram placement and spacing is paramount to a successful brand in alcohol, and right now *all brands are fighting for the refrigerated space*.

Ready to drink means....**ready to drink**! No one wants to wait for their new vodka soda to chill down. I'm. Ready. Now!

We need to talk about **craft beer** first. Cool names, local appeal, limited time only, in and out seasonality- *craft beer has it all*. Craft should be roughly 40% of your cold case. It needs to be cold and ready for consumption, full of variety and offer a multitude of "in and out" seasonal items.

The most visible trend has been the **lowering of alcohol by volume (abv)**. I know what you're saying, *give you the high test 11% and let you roam free!* Not always. You need a mix. Where everything previously was heading to high abv, we're seeing some settling. And, to put it in perspective (so you don't think I'm crazy), I'm talking 4.5% abv. If you can think back to when the "ice beers" came out, they were hovering around 4.5%, and were touted as *high alcohol content*. We've come a long way since then!

The beer types that put craft on the map has been **India Pale Ales** (or IPA's), and double IPA's and American Pale Ales (APA's). *They connected.* Sometimes, something just connects, and those styles did. IPA's are not slowing down, although the abv's are taking a turn down to something a little more handleable. We have the "juice bomb", or New England IPA, or hazy IPA's, or even unfiltered, and anything with fruit added. You put a bunch of hops in a drink, and then work your tail off to cover the hops with citrusy flavors. Inside the fruit genre, we have sours, wheats with fruit, etc.

It needs to be noted, brewmasters have been saying this for years: an IPA is one of the *least refined* ways of making beer. The massive amount of hops and alcohol can be used to cover up impurities. To a brewmaster, a perfectly brewed lager or pilsner, with reasonable alcohol content, is how you prove your craftmanship.

Quick review: most beers are either **lagers or ales**. Lagers are produced with yeast that ferments at the *bottom* of the barrel, and ales are produced with yeast that ferments at the *top* of the barrel.

Top fermenting ales are a bit less sensitive, more tolerant of alcohol, and brew at a higher temperature. **Stouts, wheat beers, and IPA's** are made with top fermenting. In ales, you find *American amber ales, American pale ales, American IPA's, Imperial IPA's (or double IPA's),* etc.

Bottom fermenting lagers are more fragile and need to ferment at a slower pace. A lager is how you show you know how to brew beer. Most **Oktoberfest** beers are lagers, same with **bocks**, and **pilsners**. Pilsner is a type of lager with a different yeast used and with hops added to it, making it hop forward. In lagers, you find *American lagers, German Helles, all pilsners, amber beers, the various bocks (doppelbock, weizenbock, maibock),* etc.

Don't forget to pay homage to the great low bitterness **Belgian beers** that put beer on the map, the super wheat beers, the beautiful porters, etc. Then, you have all the various beers with chocolate added, coffee added, fruit added, bacteria added (good bacteria), aged in wine or bourbon barrels, etc. *There is so much history in beer.*

Just remember, this is a *fickle and experimental* customer. They like to buy beer by the *type* they drink and not necessarily by the *brand*, so keep that in mind in your assortment. As soon as they like a brand, they move to another brand. Keep assortment moving in and out, so the experimenters can move around and try new things. Oh, and by the way, craft beer drinkers love *samples, events, meeting the brewers, beer shows*, etc. Be involved where these drinkers are, and you win.

And if you were wondering, *Budweiser and Coors are American lagers, Miller Lite is a pilsner, Yuengling and Sam Adams are lagers, Shiner is a bock lager (bock is German for ram, if you wanted to know why there's a ram on the label),*

Dos Equis is an amber lager, Pliny the Elder is an Imperial IPA, Blue Moon is a wheat beer, and on and on. Sometimes, walk the beer section and read the labels, it's interesting the creativity and alchemy that comes from brewmasters.

Now what? Well, we've gone crazy in two areas: **healthy and spiked "anything"**, including *seltzers and spiked teas and lemonades.* For health, once customers saw how many calories were in IPA's (some were up to 300 calories), there's been a move towards the "under 100 calories and 2.5 carbs) alternatives. *This one just took off!* Everyone got in the game! Corona Light and then Premiere, Michelob Light then Ultra then Premier, etc. A new sub-segment was born, and it's still going.

As this healthy segment was bumping up against the need to ensure females could feel as bonded to beer as males (every beer ad seemed like a bunch of guys for years!), the **hard seltzers** hit the market and took off. **White Claw** and **Truly** were market leaders. **Mike's Hard** was there before them both, and now has re-invented itself after this craze took off! And now we have **spiked everything!** Not to be outdone, we have the traditional domestic beers in the game: **Bud Light Seltzer, Natty Seltzer**, and on and on. This has truly become a cluttered section of alcoholic options! You can summarize all of the above mentioned as **flavored malt beverages (FMB's)**, as they are made by adding flavors to a malt base (same base as beer).

And, as we mentioned earlier, ready to drink spirits and ready to drink wine spritzers (like seltzers, but made with actual wine) deserve their spot in the cold case, so make sure the spacing reflects the….*customer demand.*

You can see all brands expanding into **vodka-based drinks**, including vodka in 750ml from both White Claw and Truly. The seltzer trend may be down, but the expansion of drinking options is not!

The malt beverage section is due for some fallout, as a crowded section, after a while, becomes just too much. Too many choices usually equates to **brain freeze** by customers, then they head towards simplification. Some reduction in assortment, some clarity in malt-based beverages, spirits-based, and wine-based would be good here. *Customers like simplicity.*

The Wine

Wine, other than playing in the ready to drink trend, is having a *tough time keeping customers locked in*! It's a super section, with a ton of loyalty to drinking a glass (or two or a bottle) a night, but this category needs to find a way to appeal to the next generation. A point of interest, the next generation of consumers is the *first generation that will consume more THC than alcohol*. Yes, read that one again. The next generation becoming "of age" is the first generation that will **opt for a cannabis product over an alcohol product**. And the first category being knocked out is wine.

So, yes, some re-invention is necessary here! Lock in on the **4-pack spritzer** business first. A *wine-based* 4-pack is definitely more expensive than a *malt-based* one, but price is still a secondary concern. Make it fun and exciting, and it'll gain the attraction of the younger generation. And, yes, *you're going to need to add flavors*. I know, a winemaker will faint when reading that line. Sorry, in this book we're....*customer-focused*. The next generation wants flavor forward beverages.

Rosé was a super start! Yes, I know it's been going on for years, but it showed some spunk and some excitement. Keep it going. Like white zinfandel and sangria decided to have a child. Add some rosé's with fruit in them, and make them stronger than sangria. We'll need a combination of flavor, energy and excitement, but still have an abv over 13.5%. **Flavor** is winning today. Expand out on flavor and **sweetness**. Blame it on the flavor trend, if you'd like, but sweet wines are trending quite well.

Package. Yes, *package type* is a consideration by a consumer. Besides the 4-packs mentioned, there is *high* *acceptance* of boxed wines, canned wines, and handheld little boxed wines. This trend, reflecting the improved quality of the wine in this type of packaging, the convenience of having wine available on the go, and also the freshness of having individual cans, has spurred a major real estate expansion in the category.

Not only should the section of canned and boxed wines be more elaborate than in previous years, but there needs to be a refrigerated component for the white and rosé offerings- not all of them, but a good selection. This is also where you would place the wine spritzers in 4-packs that are made with real wine.

Handheld boxes! What a convenient little item to carry with you. And! And, it's resealable. That's the issue sometimes when we're so focused on what *we* know, we rarely ask the customer what *they* want us to know. A handheld little box of wine, where you can put the cap back on, is a great little item! Play it up!

Wine varietals haven't changed much in years, neither has the merchandising of wine. When the wine is *inexpensive* (say, less than $15 for a 750ml), consumers appreciate the value of a *familiar brand*; so, we place all the brands together. A consumer can safely move within the brand with confidence.

As the wine drinker develops a palate for more *expensive* bottles (> $15 for a 750ml), they turn into more of a treasure hunt customer within their *favorite varietals* (sauvignon blanc, pinot grigio, chardonnay in whites and pinot noir, merlot, cabernet sauvignon, red zinfandel, grenache, syrah in reds (plus some variations and blends in both)). So, we focus more on a varietal set and move labels in and out.

If you choked on your grape when **flavor** was mentioned, then hopefully you cleared your throat by now. A *customer-focused* company looks at trends and talks with customers about what *they* want.   Right now, the customer wants fun, flavor, convenience, and a little bit of zippiness to their drinking experience. Somewhere there is a gin or vodka master distiller who sat back and thought *"hey, no way will I add flavors to my product! There's no way I will go down that road. I'm a purist!"*.

You know what that person is doing today?   *I don't either*. Customers have a funny way of asking you to come along. They're going a certain direction no matter what, you can come along or watch the caboose as it fades into the sunset.

The Spirits

As the last of the three major types of alcohol, **spirits** have done a fantastic job re-inventing themselves! Honestly, this category had been left in the boneyard with the armadillos and tumbleweed. No longer the "old person pouring scotch at 5:00 before going to bed at 7:00" category, we now have *vibrant colors, flavors, small batches, large batches, hot locations (think Austin!), and a slew of new ready to drink options.* Like the phoenix, spirits have come back to life! Let's talk about a few areas.

Vodka and Gin. Good ole vodka and gin. Like the siblings that grow up and are "same, but different". Both are fermented, then distilled. Both can be made with potatoes, rye, corn, even grapes and carrots. It's the flavor and the *water* setting them apart. In *gin's* case, you then add juniper and flavors. In *vodka's* case, you're trying for the neutral template, so it can be used as a mixer with whatever flavor you choose. Once distilled multiple times, you add water back in to bring the abv to 40%. *Water quality becomes the distinguishing factor in the tastes.*

Some spirits, like vodka, were *already trending up*. Vodka has a slew of new botanical-infused offers, but then also has the "Tito's effect", where Tito's became ubiquitous in recent years, then Deep Eddy, and on and on. This is where vodka and gin separate on the railroad tracks. **Vodka** seems to have the upper-hand in uniqueness and innovation, as well as playing up location-specific differences. Remember, this isn't like a grape that must be grown in a region, *you can make vodka and gin anywhere*; so, it's all in the marketing. Tell your story better, and you win. Tito's uses corn from Indiana, they just don't talk about it. The message of "handmade in Texas" is what works. Defining "handmade" is like defining bottled water's "bottled at the source". What does that really mean?

The additional trend here is in the **mixers**, especially **ginger beer**. Holy cow, ginger beer has exploded in popularity! It seems everyone is making some sort of Moscow Mule, and might not even know it. Make a section with **ginger beer, lime juice, triple sec, alcohol-infused olives**, etc. This is a fun addition to the category, and elicits the alchemist in all of us. And it's ginger, it must be healthy!

Whiskey! Adding to the vodka trend is whiskey. Thanks, Eric Church. Or, should I say "whisky". Whiskey (and whisky) are on fire, both figuratively and literally! Yes, adding *cinnamon* to whiskey is hot, and it started with **Fireball** (whisky). **Jack Daniels** (whiskey, *or is it Kentucky Bourbon*) didn't want to miss the craze, so there's Jack Fire (plus honey, apple, etc.). What a fun category! Flavors, single batch, single barrel, multi barrel, etc. This category has everything going for it. *Fuel the fire* in whiskey.

Closely related, **bourbon** is also rising, but is still seen as an "older person" drink, so some re-invention needs to happen here. The issue with bourbon is the good stuff costs *so darn much*. The price makes it either inaccessible to a large portion of the population, or too risky to try at that price. Put **scotch** in this slot, too. Tell me the last time you heard any young person ask for a scotch? I'll wait.

Tequila and mezcal. Another "same, but different" pair of siblings. Both come from the core of the *agave plant*, but tequila is produced by steaming the agave in *industrial ovens*, while mezcal is traditionally cooked in *earthen pits*- although it's difficult to produce a lot of product by earthen pit cooking, so this is becoming more industrialized. *Tequila* has three types (blanco, reposado, and anejo), which represent length of aging time. *Mezcal* took the same route, except uses joven in place of blanco. Both, though, have a reputation for low calories and are seen as "healthy". They're a healthier choice *in alcohol*, maybe not necessarily healthy. **Honestly, the healthiest alcohol is still red wine, as long as pesticides aren't coming along for the ride.**

As we discussed earlier, **ready to drink (RTD) spirits** are where it's at! These days, you can find any mixture of spirits already mixed in a can and ready to drink (thus, the name). And it's highly appealing to customers to see these high abv RTD spirits sitting in <u>refrigeration</u>. Being able to drink a **Moscow Mule** or a **lemon vodka**, without needing to bring out the bottle of vodka, lime juice, lemon juice, ginger beer, etc. is a time utility provided by RTD's. Keep focusing on this segment, and the customer will continue rewarding you with sales.

We do not see alcohol trending down any time soon. In fact, the biggest trend that could hurt alcohol sales? **THC legalization**. As we discussed, legalizing marijuana has shown an impact on alcohol sales, primarily due to the younger generation of consumers finding THC as a viable choice for relaxation. Just something to watch.

Overall, *alcohol is on a tear!* Keep up with, and stay ahead of, the customers! They're fickle, treasure-hunt oriented, and are showing signs of continuing the upward trend for the foreseeable future.

The Center Store

We've been walking the perimeter of the store, and now let's head to the center of the store. We usually call this area the....**center store** (we're simple folk here!). For overall image of freshness and abundance, the fresh departments we just covered are the drivers. For overall reputation of *assortment and fulfilling the needs of every shopper* to feed themselves and/or their families, center store is the center of attention.

All areas of the store feed off each other (yes, I said that in a food book). Where a store that sold only meat and produce would be fun to stop by *once in a while*, it wouldn't fulfill all your needs. Vice versa, a center store without super fresh departments, also will not fulfill all your needs. It's why you go to the farmer's market and walk around, but *still need to go shopping for "regular" food later.*

There are a few overall keys here that apply to the entire center store. Understand the **traffic flow** (which way the customers normally traverse your store) and ensure you have an opinion on traffic flow and adjacencies by category. In general, though, your *upsell* and *higher margin rate* items should be eye level and first in traffic flow. The higher volume items should be on the bottom shelf for inventory holding power, where you'll have a better chance of being in stock throughout the day. The **higher volume items**, since they need to be competitively priced (and less margin rate), aren't necessarily the first items you want a customer to consider. They'll find the ketchup on their list, they won't always find the locally made special sauce- let them see the unique item first.

You should make an effort to consider the **consumer decision tree** (CDT) for each category, as in which decision is most important to the majority of the customers (price? brand? flavor?), then second decision, and so on. For example, coffee, most customers know the form they want first (Keurig machines versus other coffee machines, or wanting whole beans, etc.), then decaf or caffeinated, then flavor. As they scan the shelf, you can make it easier for them to find what they want if you attempt to follow *their decision making process*. The CDT is one of the most important aspects of relating your shelving and assortment to the customer's expectation.

As always, remember customer first and you'll be okay. Let's go up and down the aisles.

One point here, I'm going to focus on *trends*, and break them up by **beverages** and **food**. Not all categories have changed much in the last few years, where other categories have had an *unbelievable amount of change*. All of it customer-driven. That's where we'll focus. You don't need a book to tell you to put syrup next to pancake mix. Hopefully.

Inflation Tips: Sounding like a broken record here, but we need to help our customers be able to afford life, and smaller packs sizes can do that. It's not cheating the customer (yes, the media calls it shrinkflation), it's making things affordable. The entire dollar store model is based upon this premise.

The Beverages

We're going to start in the **beverage aisle**. The beverage aisle has exploded into "everything in liquid form" over the last few years. There is no end in sight. Of course, you still need **carbonated soft drinks**. They're not on a positive trend, but they're not going away either. The splitting of Coke and Pepsi and all their usual line-up of diet and yellow (Mountain Dew) and green (Sprite) and everything in between makes sense, and the customers expect it to be organized in this manner. The little cans, the Coke from Mexico with real sugar, etc. are all part of the normal offer.

One magical item is the *24-pack cube of soft drinks*. As a rule, I'd suggest you keep cubes of soft drinks on the sales floor at all times. They are magical. Even when two 12-packs would be cheaper, customers *still buy the cubes*. Not sure why, but whatever makes them happy.

Where beverages *have* split off, though, is in the **everything else** category, which includes....everything else. You need to take control of this explosion of products and help the customer make some sense of it all. And, to make it even more complicated you have "real" and "fake" products. You have real tea, like from **Ito En**, and you have sugary tea from **Arnold Palmer**. Then, you have "energy" drinks like **Red Bull** and you have "energy plus" drinks like **Monster** or **Bang** or any of those power sounding drinks.

And what do you do with **Celsius, Bubly, Bubbl'r, Bai**, etc.? These are alternatively tea-based, water-based, juice-based drinks that tout their DBA's (distinctive brand attributes, if you skipped the first part of this book).

In case you were starting to make sense of it all, many of these products are great for **instant consumption** (so they need refrigeration) and many are for **stock-up** at home. What do you do? The jury is still out, especially when you have mass confusion, like **Starbuck's** brand on items that *look like* coffee and items like **Super Coffee** that *are* actual coffee sweetened with MCT oil. The best suggestion is let it play out for a while. Stick with the "Red Bull-like" products near the Coke and Pepsi, and try to make some organization between **fruit drinks, superberry drinks, real tea drinks, sugar drinks**, and oh yeah....**bottled water**.

Water needs to be near these other drinks, but it has multiple uses that must be acknowledged. Some cities simply have bad water. In those areas, a 24-pack of single-use bottled water is not the solution. You need larger packs, and larger sizes in those packs, including a water machine. In other areas, like resort areas or anywhere in the south, you have heavy consumption of bottled water for individual hydration. No one said this was going to be easy, did they?

What's new in this aisle, though? Here's a question for you, what's **Pedialyte** used for? If you answered something about babies, you're only partially correct. Go to Walgreens in Las Vegas and look at the endcaps of Pedialyte. Now, look around at all the babies....*there aren't any*. Re-purposing electrolyte drinks as a *hangover cure* is one of the more brilliant re-branding initiatives of the last few years. And now **Gatorade** (including **Gatorlyte**) has introduced new products, mainly because they were first on the electrolyte market, and need to protect their turf!

A suggestion, a radical suggestion....either *move the Pedialyte products into the beverage aisle*, or at least place them in both Health and Beauty Care (HBC) *and* the beverage aisle. Or, place them near the alcohol section. Remember, customer-focus first. Like red Solo cups and ping pong balls in the alcohol section. There's no need to act like we don't know what customers are doing.

Coffee is trending like crazy, in all areas: ready to drink, drink in store, drive-through, make at home, frozen drinks, even added to beer. If you want to make an impact in a category, this one is a pretty sure bet. Like pizza, there is always demand for coffee, you just need to *take the customers from someone else*. Plus, also like pizza, customers have shown an amazing ability to consume everything you put in front of them. People see a Starbuck's and they start to salivate (for real), **so why not offer coffee bars in the stores, and go big**? You're going to need to address **olive oil coffee**. Love or hate Starbuck's, but they are ubiquitous enough to start a trend, and olive oil coffee is their latest.

Make them *coffee and tea bars*, stock your coffee and tea aisle adjacent to the coffee and tea bar, give some outside or inside seating, make sure your wi-fi is strong, *really play this up*! And, if you can locate the coffee and tea bar near the perimeter of the store, then you can offer drive-through and pick-up. The trend shows no signs of slowing. And if you don't have room, try **coffee kiosks** in your parking lot. You have got to make sure you capture as much coffee business as possible, and customers are showing no signs of slowing.

Speaking of **tea**, the same trends in coffee are even stronger in tea. *Ready to drink, make at home, experimental, trial*, they are all showing solid trends. Yup, another healthy item on fire. The variety seems to have no end. Think of how informed the customers are today. Most people previously only knew black tea. Now, they look for green, white, chai green, matcha, chai white, orange, pu-erh, and on and on. Keep a special eye on anything with **turmeric or ginger**. They are rocking flavors right now!

How do you organize all this? If you step back and look at all the non-alcoholic beverages in the store, you can come to some sort of categorization, in the sense you have **soft drinks and energy drinks**- with a blurry line between them (made even more blurry with Coke Energy); then you have juice-based drinks- which may or may not be related to superberries; then you have **coffee and tea**-based drinks- which may or may not contain coffee or tea; then you have the other varieties- like **aloe drinks**; then you have the **fermented drinks**- like kombucha; and you have the **meal substitute** drinks- like Carnation Breakfast and Ensure; and you have **drinkable yogurt and kefir**; then you have drinks that *caffeinate* you to the sky and drinks that put you to *sleep*. It keeps expanding exponentially. At least acknowledge drinks have some sort of "base" ingredient, so you can help the customer make decisions.

The customers are showing they love beverages, so don't back off. It's not like they aren't making decisions, look at how much cranberry and grape juice has *shrunk* the last five years, but the space for beverages has *expanded*. This is like squeezing a balloon. As one area declines in popularity, another expands. The point is, customers lead the way, and we're here to take care of them.

Inflation Tips: One tip in this section is to make multi-packs more accessible price-wise. Give a much better price on multi-packs, so the customer sees the value. And one word of warning, it's easy for a customer to fulfill their needs for drinks they consumer every day on either Amazon or ordering directly from the manufacturer. That's not bad, per se, just make sure you know how customers think.

The Food

We'll talk about a variety of the center store **food** areas. Like I said at the beginning, the focus will be more on trendy areas, and less on categories that are stable. Technically, this section is anything in the center store you *don't drink*.

Okay, here's a question for you? **Where's the bar?** No, not that one. Where do you find **protein bars**? Where do you find **meal replacement bars**? What if you want **Rx Bars**? What about **Atkins**? The answer to all these questions remains....*I have no idea*. Yes, we have totally confused the customer on this one. You can find Quest, Pure Protein, Atkins, WW, etc. in the *HBC aisle*. You can find Rx Bars, Luna, Kind, etc. in the *center store*. And what about the OG granola bars, and what about Dipps? Are they candy or protein? And what to do with Belvita? Been asking that for years!

I'd suggest the customer would appreciate **one spot with all bars**. Stop letting how you *procure* the product dictate where you *shelve* the product. Unless you have a dietitian on staff who will evaluate every bar you offer in the store, and categorize by health benefits, the best bet is to let the customers decide. **But!** But, *put them all in one spot*. And, make sure you offer a competitive value on multi-packs.

Here's a secret, the customer isn't telling you they're confused. *They're just going somewhere else.* Try typing in pureprotein.com, and you'll see some great offers for multi-packs; plus, reduced prices on continuous *subscriptions* of product. Every customer who signs up for a subscription directly from the manufacturer is gone from your store. *Forever.* When it comes to protecting your turf, the only choice is to come out swinging!

Snacking packs. Similar to bar proliferation, snacking packs are *everywhere*. I'm purposely calling them *snacking packs*, not *snack packs*. I want to reflect the broader purpose of these packs. As opposed to protein bars, I'm not suggesting these should be combined, solely suggesting they be *acknowledged as a trend*. There are snacking packs in refrigerated, as we already discussed; but there are also snacking packs in the snack section, packs in the jerky section, snacking packs in cereal, snacking packs in breakfast, etc. Just watch them, and make sure to understand where the customer is going.

To add on to snacking packs, let's talk about traditional **snacks**. I'm going to combine **salty snacks** and **cookies and crackers**, and include **jerky**. The primary utility provided by all these items is to snack, *right*? And, switchability? It's high amongst sub-categories. You cannot substitute an **Oreo** for a **Tostito**, but you could potentially substitute a **Chips Ahoy** for an Oreo, or a different corn salty item for a Tostito.

Let's add **multi-packs** to the trend, as we discussed earlier. In fact multi-packs of snack packs is where it started, before multi-packs took off everywhere! Join the multi-pack revolution.

Once again, if you look at these categories from the customer's perspective, you have categories that can be organized in a few different ways: **salty snacks**, with corn tortilla base or potato base or cheese base; then **pretzels**, with a million different ways to form a pretzel; then the **vegetable-based** products, which may or may not contain vegetables; and then those perfectly shaped potato products called **Pringle's** (and Lay's Stax). Watch for **chicken skins** to join **pork skins** in this section.

Then, on the cookie and cracker side, you have the thousand different ways to make a **chocolate chip cookie**, then the **Nilla Wafer** section, then the various types of

crackers- some (like graham) to be eaten straight, and some to be used as carriers of cheese, spreads, or whatever you can place on them.

Then there's the hot one- **jerky**. Oh boy, everything is in jerky form now! *Salmon, beef, turkey, buffalo, mushrooms, pork, plant-based*, etc. Everything can be "jerkied", and it's all selling. The *inflation tip* here is jerky tends to be expensive. Smaller packs of jerky can help the customers. The convenience of an item that doesn't need refrigeration, can last forever (figuratively) is what's making it attractive to consumers. Take care of this section, and continue to expand the space.

Look for **sea floss, kelp, seaweed, yuzu, and ube** flavors to trend in the snacking section this year.

For snacking, *think like a customer*, and understand your definition of brand loyalty may not equate to the customer's definition of utility and value provided by snacks. Focus on being in-stock, then allow for a "better for you" section of organics, plant-based, etc. Humans will always snack. It happens. Be there for them, and offer a large variety.

One other area exploding is the **snacking nuts** section. There are so many different ways to package a nut, and a ton of different levels of roasting and salting them, and there seems to be a customer for *every level and every mixture*. Almost every customer is trained to look for the nuts they are searching for in the snack section first; then, if they cannot find them, they go to the baking nuts section to look for them. It's possible we could eliminate some confusion by having a "nut world" somewhere in between the snacking aisle and the baking aisle. One hot trend are the **shelled pistachios**. What was previously a fun thing to do, shell each pistachio, is now a pain in the arse. Along come shelled pistachios. They really are hot!

While we're in a snacking mood, let's talk **chocolate and candy**. Think of these as two separate areas, and two distinct customers. On one hand, you have the "normal" candy sections of **peanut-based, non-peanut, chocolate-enrobed everything, non-chocolate**, etc. This area shows innovation by using the same known name brand item and adding new spring flavors, fall flavors, etc. Hey, why not? You know **M&M's**, so why not try caramel M&M's? And **Reese's**, oh my goodness! The candy section is almost all "Reese's orange" these days! Also, why not? *How can you not love Reese's?* I'd pick Reese's for breakfast and lunch, with pizza for dinner. *The perfect day.*

In addition, you have the explosion of **dark chocolate** as a healthy item in most diets. And, because it's attracted a health-oriented crowd, you have a gushing fountain of *organic, free trade, various levels of cacao, varying levels of sweet and bitter, addition of all types of fruit flavors, and then various forms*. You have the traditional bars, like **Lily's** and **Justin's**, and then you have the on-the-go snack bags, like **Brookfield**.

All snack and candy items are *expandable consumable*, as in "the more you have at home, the more you consume". It's going to be difficult to corral and channel the growth in innovation and variety in candy and chocolate, but improved organization to the sets would make sense, and help the customers make decisions.

Now that we've had our dessert first, let's talk about the meal. *Affordable eating and stretching meals* are going to be the top actions in inflationary times, and the center store is perfectly situated. Let's talk **pasta, noodles, ramen, rice**, etc. You may think it sounds like Depression Era eating, because it kind of is, you know? When you're tight on money in inflationary times, or a college student, *ramen and pasta are your best friend!*

If there are any items that stretch a budget, it's a **carb** that can feed many people. Think of most meals in this world, they consist of putting some type of protein in/on/or surrounded by a carb. It's the way the world works. Not suggesting anything new for this section except keep it in-stock and keep trying new things. New **soba or udon** noodles from Japan, **bronze cut pasta** from Italy, **sweet potato pasta**, even higher quality **ramen** than the college-staple ramen, really anything you can do to help customers make it through inflation.

Speaking of inflation, **canned meats** are still hot. **Canned fish** had quite a trend as a clean way to introduce small fish with high omega-6's into your diet, like **mackerel and sardines.** Still some of the best fish for you, but the trend has leveled. And remember snacking packs, *tuna is still the leader in canned fish, when you consider snacking packs.* Then in the "other meat", well, you've got **SPAM**. SPAM enjoyed a nice resurgence the last few years, and it's not slowing down. It's SPAM. *A tradition like no other.* SPAM musubis are so much fun to try at home, it's worth it to talk them up in your stores.

Baking! Talk about a category left to die that came back to life in a big way! So many people renewed their joy, or discovered a new joy, for cooking and baking the last few years! As the chefs say, *"be creative while cooking, stick to the rules in baking".* The rigidity of baking is appealing to people. The fact you must follow the directions is kind of relaxing. And when you get that *one perfect loaf of bread?* *Magic!* There are a few areas in this section that have seen the most impact- **yeast and flour, spices, healthy coatings, and nature-based sugar alternatives, like monkfruit and MCT oil.**

Spices are on fire! All of them. As part of the health and cooking kick, customers have realized that spices are *pretty darn good for you.* An informed customer is using turmeric for anti-inflammation, using **cloves** for digestion, using **cayenne** for metabolism, **cinnamon** for everything, **garlic** for vampires, etc. And the list goes on. The beauty of the spice category is there is *so much variety*. So, keep up with variety, keep up with health food sites, keep up with social media where people talk about how they cook, and this category is going to be on fire for a while!

There is also an intermix here between **spices and sauces**. Especially, as you might imagine, *sauces made with spices*. We've talked about **turmeric** a number of times, definitely the star of the last few years. We also need to understand how Asian spices and broths play into what people are buying in this section. **Piri piri sauce, Lao Gan Ma, Za'atar, sriracha, and gochujang** are seriously coming into their own in Western diets. And, while you're at it, don't forget all the various forms of **curry**, almost all including....turmeric.

And **broths**? Another area where baking and broths and cultures are combining beautifully. **Bone broth** is much more expensive than "regular" broths, and is *significantly better for you*. Adding spices to bone broths is a way to seem like you are preparing a "homemade broth", but much easier. It, of course, brings up another question: where do you put the **sipping bone broths**? Sipping bone broth is a trend. The best place for the broths is to have them all together in the baking aisle, and adjacent to the soup aisle.

What else is going on in center store? How about everything **Truff**? What a hot little brand of truffled-infused hot sauce, and now pasta sauce. Ride it while you can. A bit expensive, but something new to try. Anything by **Momofuku** is hot. A testament to the power of a restaurant name, and how it pervades consumer goods on the shelf. **Fancy mustards** have had a comeback, led by anything with Dijon or whole grain and whole seed. **Prebiotic** and anything probiotic. Say *microbiome*, and you catch the attention of most shoppers. I'd say cauliflower pastas and crusts, but....*I just can't stand cauliflower.* I've yet to find anything made with cauliflower that tastes good....including cauliflower. If you're a cauliflower grower and are offended. *Sorry.* It's my book, and I have an opinion.

Cereal. This aisle is absolutely crazy. As I pick up my new Little Debbie Oatmeal Pie cereal, I'd have to wonder why we need all of this assortment. Once again, if you look at it from the customer's point of view, you have **healthy** and **not healthy**, and in many forms and sizes. This is not to say innovation is bad. It is to say, though, we may not need five different sizes of Cheerios and eight different flavors. And, if you're going to get rid of either sizes or flavors, make it the sizes.

A radical idea, how about a **breakfast solution** area in the store, so all breakfast options can be explored by the customers? And, instead of a *cereal* CDT, how about a *breakfast* CDT? That way, a customer can pick and choose based upon their circumstances. As retailers and consumer packaged goods companies, you need to choose the customer first over what you might need for your current assortment. If in the end the customer does not want your current offering, develop (or buy) what they want.

For the most part, the large companies in this space have done an excellent job expanding into breakfast bars and other solutions- they just forgot to suggest which items in boxed cereal *need to be deleted.* That is why we do not have enough variety in healthy oatmeal, overnight oat prep areas, keto products, healthy pancake solutions, etc. There's no room.

When one segment needs almost two sides of an entire aisle for its assortment, *it has too much assortment.* Customers want your help! When Aldi can carry forty cereal items and their stores are expanding like crazy, do you really think you need four to five hundred sku's of cereal? And this is not to hurt the major manufacturers of cereal. In fact, it would help efficiencies if the volume could be pumped into fewer items.

And **Pop Tarts**! You know, there are *very few items* where no one has been able to put up a good fight against them, and you can count them on one hand: Gatorade, Pringles (yes, I like Stax, but still), Totino's pizza rolls, Dorito's, and Pop Tarts. *No one can touch Pop Tarts*. You have got to respect the power of Pop Tarts, and ride any new trends they bring. You really have no choice.

How about **bread**? I'm not a big fan of the bread aisle being combined into the bakery, as some stores have done. Customers do not think that way, and you just confuse them. When you do have the bread aisle in the *regular aisles* of the store, you can have the same bountiful selection of types of breads, varying levels of healthiness, dinner rolls, tortillas, hamburger and hot dog buns, and even pita breads.

An area to look for here is ensuring the **healthy breads**, the ones that are *actually healthy*, have a prominent spot in the aisle. Make sure the ones called healthy, but still loaded with sugar, salt, and high fructose corn syrup, are located in the traffic flow by the snack cakes. That's what they are. **Thin sliced, whole grain breads** are having their moment, and are sometimes squeezed out by the white breads. If you were to find a picture of the bread aisle ten or fifteen years ago, it would have been dominated by white bread. No longer!

And, yes, the age old question of where to house the **peanut butter and jelly** should be answered here. Right here, next to their best friend- *bread*. PB&J as an adjacency to bread is expected by the customer. And, inside PB&J, keep in mind the need for *organics, natural, real peanut butter and jelly*. Peanut butter, especially, has been morphed and altered so many different ways! Sometimes actual peanuts are not even the top listed ingredient! Bread, and it's close friends PB&J and snack cakes, have a super connection in the eyes of the customer. They are family. Keep the family together.

There are new trends and food segments popping up continuously, like anything **keto, healthy popcorns, salts from around the world, immunity shots, restaurant pastas (think tagliatelle), anything microbiome, anything containing ginger and turmeric, and anything around health and immune system boosting**. Environmental scanning is the key to knowing where the customer is going, and getting there ahead of them- and ahead of the competition.

Inflation Tips: We've covered too many categories for any over-arching inflation tips, other than think of the customer first, and always. Customers don't make government fiscal policies, have nothing to do with interest rates, cannot control Saudi Arabia's oil output, and are just trying to live their lives and take care of their families. We're here to try and help. It's tough out there!

The Nonfoods

The **nonfoods** section of the center store has been the story of the last few years, due to the ability to *clean things*, or because the *supply chain couldn't keep up*. Other than that, we do have a few categories to discuss, but it'll be short.

Antibacterial wipes. The story of the last few years. We seem to be back to normal in this area. In fact, it's seeming like "back to normal" means no one cleans anything anymore. Even the **Seventh Generation** product is selling again.

Paper Towels and Bath Tissue and Laundry Detergent. Other than keeping them in stock, and having a variety of one-ply all the way to four-ply, this category is *in need of organization*. But how? Who really knows? The different pricing and sizing and "sheets per roll" have made it an incredibly confusing category for customers to shop and compute value. Customers have adjusted and just trust that anything on display is a value. Not sure that's such a bad thing.

I included **laundry detergent** in here for the same reason as towels and tissue. The customer is so confused by number of loads and ultra versus premium versus regular, they tend to trust *anything on display is a value*. The focus has returned to how detergents and cleaners impact our health and the earth, so eliminating harmful chemicals has become the re-focus.

Other than those main areas, nonfood is stable, in the sense that not much has changed in twenty years. You still need **storage bags** that can withstand the freezer, and **storage bags** that can hold a sandwich. You need **aluminum foil** that can withstand a grill and **plastic wrap** that can *not* *wrap the first time and frustrate you to no end!!!!* And, yes, it's good when **disposable plates and cups** hold drinks and food.

Brooms and mops and Swiffer products, buckets and sponges and cleaning accessories. All essential, all necessary, and all have at least three tiers of quality: opening price point, national brand, and value added (or high end).

Let's move on to *drugs....*

The Beauty and Drugs

As we finish our walk of the store, we round the corner into the **health and beauty care (HBC)** section. If there were ever a confusing section of the store, it would be this one! *This is cereal times 1,000!* Have you ever had a horrible headache and stood in front of the pain relievers and *your headache got worse* as you tried to figure them out? Do I need a tension or a migraine solution? Do I want caffeine in it, or not? Will the store brand work as well as the name brand? Did I read acetaminophen was good for me or bad for me? Did I hear I should not mix ibuprofen and aspirin? Is this going to put me to sleep or make me jittery? Why do they sell ibuprofen in 1,000 tablet jars? Does that mean it must be safe for my stomach? **I'm. So. Confused!**

I know what I'll do, I'll just brush my teeth and go to bed. I just need **toothpaste**. Let me head over there.... Ahhhhhhhhhh!!!!!!!!! *Why are there so many toothpastes?* And, while we're at it, why are there so many mouthwashes and shampoos and conditioners and body washes and soap *for men* and soap *for women* and soft toothbrushes and hard toothbrushes and a whole bunch of products in case I feel incontinent right here in the aisle? *If I weren't incontinent before I entered this aisle, that's changed.*

The main idea in this area of the store is these items are usually an **immediate necessity** (my head!), a **personal and private choice** (do I want Trojan or Durex?), or are for **someone else** (you were the only one healthy enough to go to the store). Organize it all in a way that you are over-communicating the uses and the types to the customer. If you think of it as we do specialty wines or cheeses, you'd be thinking *customer-first*. Plus, if you reminded the customer they could order online (even give them a QR code in-aisle) and the personal and private products would arrive in a little brown box at their front door, you could stop the sales erosion to online ordering from Amazon, Walmart, and Target. *Do you really think anyone wants to stand in line at the front checkout with a big box of **Depends** and risk a price check?*

De-sku, communicate the differences in the products, make it private and personal, and offer online options in a simple manner.

One note, items proclaiming they are **immunity boosters** are going to be popular for quite a while. Emergen-C and all those vitamin C's and D's make sense, if the product actually works. Since you are not in the efficacy testing business, just carry them. And newness? **Mushroom extracts, chlorophyll tablets**, etc. *Trends are constantly flowing through this section like flax.*

Health and beauty is an interesting section, driven by immediate need, the majority of the time. Matching up the *customer's need* with *simplifying their shopping experience* could pay out in spades. You will need to make a decision, though, on *where to shelve nutrition powders, nutrition bars*, etc. Target has them split, with bars in the snack aisle and powders in the pharmacy area. Walmart has them all together in health and beauty care. Just make a decision and stick with it. Not sure the first thought when about to head to the gym and needing a protein powder is to walk to the pharmacy.

Should you carry CBD?

I've written three books on **Cannabidiol (CBD)** and the other cannabinoids from the cannabis plant, including up and comers **Cannabigerol (CBG) and Cannabinol (CBN)**. By most indications, the stigma that might have been present with these products has vanished in favor of the fact *they tend to work.*

Then, you have the federal legalization of the big dog, **Tetrahydrocannabinol (THC)**, or the cannabinoid coming from the cannabis plant that connects with the CB1 connector in your Endocannabinoid System (ECS), and sometimes impairs motor skills (CBD comes from hemp, has less than .3% THC, and actually blocks any connections to the CB1 connector, only bonding with the CB2. For the purposes of the grocery stores, we are only talking about **CBD** products, and the other cannabinoids that are *not THC.* Unless you open your own dispensary, you cannot carry THC.

But, you *can* carry CBD, and I'd suggest you get into it in a big way. It's showing no signs of slowing, and is becoming a go-to natural solution for inflammation, insomnia, and assorted pain (remember that bottle of 1,000 ibuprofen pills?).

That's all I'll say about CBD. I have three other books you can read about CBD, including the latest *The ABC's of THC and CBD*, available on Amazon in over 25 countries☺

The Pricing

We've walked this big beautiful place we call the grocery store, we've talked about trends and customers and assortment, and now one more thing: **pricing**.

A number of years ago, we published a strategy in the *Journal of Food Products Marketing* that covered the topic of traditional food stores using their store brands program for an **everyday low price** component, to enhance their service and customer engagement strengths. To read the entire article, see Everyday Low Pricing: A Private Brand Growth Strategy in Traditional Food Retailers in *Journal of Food Products Marketing*, 24(10), pp. 1-19. To summarize some key findings, though, here is what we found. If you are struggling to find a way to compete against the price operators, this is a proven strategy that is affordable for most traditional retailers.

The suggestion: If we move the pricing of our store brands program to everyday low price, and then communicate those prices, we will see a sales increase at a higher rate than the national brands versus last year.

The store brands EDLP test was to address the needs for a traditional food retailer to have a viable strategy versus everyday low price operators, without diminishing its identity as a promotional retailer. In addition, the intrinsic benefits that come from store brands growth should increase customer loyalty and repeat visits, without a tremendous hit to margin rate- ostensibly building a barrier to entry around the retailer versus the competition.

The study aimed to expand the domain of store brands strategies by including a broader sales growth role than is normally found in the branding literature, particularly using store brands as a centerpiece of growth and not solely as a less expensive option to national brands.

The results prompted program adoption. The results were significant enough for the retailer in the study to adopt the pricing model permanently. It suggests that successful food retailers explore pricing models different from their preferred format to enhance sales growth. The study also suggests a link between traditional "mass merchant categories" (those categories offered at everyday low price in mass merchants-household, paper goods, cereal) and growth through everyday low pricing.

Even considering the various unknowns, we believe we can suggest specific inferences for store brand pricing in highly promotional food retailers. "Mass merchant" categories may show a positive increase in sales through an everyday low price component being added to the marketing mix. Paper goods, household, detergent, and staple everyday categories can benefit from a consistently low price available the entire month on certain sku's. Heavily promoted categories could react favorably to an everyday low price component. In this specific study, cold cereal responded extremely well (best in the study) to an everyday low price grouping of sku's being "brand blocked" in the cereal aisle.

This study showed traditional retailers can win the price game in a highly competitive market, while maintaining what makes them special- their service and engagement- their people. Do it! Your customers will love you for it!

Today's Store Walk

Today's Store Walk. A walk through a store today, in today's environment of treasure hunt versus inflation, commodity needs versus the need for experiences, health and wellness needs versus affordability. The beauty of the grocery store is **it's all there**! Inside those four walls is a beautiful and bountiful offering of the greatest food assortment our world has to offer.

We're fortunate to be involved in this industry! An industry that feeds people, helps them celebrate, commemorates graduations and deaths, brings people together for weddings, and provides the ice cream and margaritas for the divorces. We're there every step of the way. The fortunate few who grow up in this business are the lucky ones!

From one lucky one to another, I hope you've enjoyed this book!

~ Dr. Z

About Dr. Z

It all started when I was fourteen. I can remember the day like it was yesterday. I received a call on the phone that was connected to the wall, and picked up the receiver that was connected by a cord to the phone connected to the wall- (giving you a little insight into the timing and my age). And, surprise to anyone under twenty years of age, we did not know who was calling. That little bit of technology would come later. It was my brother, Warren, on the other line. He was calling from Fogle's Food City in West Columbia, South Carolina. Warren worked in the produce department, and wanted to know if I could come down and work a few shifts while the older teenagers went to the beach.

Warren had gotten his job because our oldest brother, Merrill, had referred him. In fact, pretty much everyone working at Fogle's Food City had gotten the job because someone in their family had previously worked there. It's what you did in the small independent operators, much like still happens today in stores all over the world. The job? Bag groceries, take them to the customers' cars, and pocket the tips. I would work for tips plus $2.25 per hour, paid with cash from the register. I was underage, after all.

So, that started what was going to be a super career in the food industry. But, I didn't know it at the time. In fact, once I became of "legal age" and took my rightful place replacing Warren as the "assistant produce clerk" in a department of two of us, the industry was already changing rapidly. Looking back now, the industry has always been changing rapidly. My Produce Manager at the time, Forrest, taught me one of my first lessons in food. When I asked him how to pick out the best watermelon, he told me simply- "tap three and pick the middle one". That little tidbit of wisdom had deeper meaning, and was more prescient, than Forrest probably even knew.

First, **customers are constantly searching for knowledge and insight into what they should eat**. Second, **they seem to trust anyone who acts like they know what they are doing**. The responsibility to take food nutritional guidelines, safety procedures, contamination control, etc. seriously weighs on the merchant or the food purveyor. There is an inherent trust in those who hand us our food. Whatever life lessons I learned, they didn't matter, I was going to the University of South Carolina and majoring in Engineering. I would keep the job until I graduated and would then get a "real job". After a semester in Engineering, I realized quickly that I needed to find another major. Choosing Psychology as my major, I still had plans to graduate and get the heck out of this grocery business.

One more lesson from Fogle's Food City before we move on. A lesson in consolidation and just how **tight the margins** are in food retail. Fogle's, owned by Bobby Fogle in Neese's, South Carolina (home of the best liver mush in the world....if you like that kind of stuff), was supplied by Thomas and Howard. Thomas and Howard, like many voluntary wholesalers (a term used to describe the supplier relationship between the retailer and the wholesaler) had an inherent desire to want to be paid when they shipped goods to retailers like Fogle's. The basis of marketing is exchange, remember? Two parties exchange something of value so that both parties are better off after the transaction. Well, in this case, Fogle's was running out of their side of the exchange equation- the cash side.

Wholesalers exist because small independents, like Fogle's Food City at the time, are not large enough to buy the goods they sell at the best price on their own. They need a *wholesaler to link them together and buy for them. In exchange for a fee, the wholesaler buys the goods from the major consumer packaged goods companies at the best bracket price, holds those goods in inventory, and ships them to the retailers when the retailer needs them.*

Over time, though, independents sometimes run short of cash, cannot pay their supplier, and then either must sell the operation to someone else, go bankrupt, or be bought by their supplier. Fogle's was eventually bought by Thomas and Howard, became a Giant Food World, then became a furniture store, and is now well- I have no idea what is there. It wasn't the best area of town. The Fogle's Store Manager through most of my time there, Keith, had a saying, "Ain't nothing but a thing". I never was quite sure what he meant by that, but he was a great guy who left every day with the phrase, "I'm going home to have a cold beer." Small independent stores are filled with some of the best people in the industry.

By the time Fogle's became a furniture store, I had moved on to work at BI-LO. My first job? Night stocker. If you have never experienced the "opportunity" to work third shift in any capacity, you haven't missed much. Probably one of the worst jobs ever. I guess I could have been cleaning porta potties on third shift….maybe that would be the worst job ever.

Anyway, the big shiny BI-LO was where I was going to call home for the next five to six years. At Fogle's, I had worked in every department from grinding meat to baking doughnuts. These experiences would come in handy at BI-LO. What can you learn at a corporate store like BI-LO? A lot! My Store Manager at the time, Bob, was a gnarly, irascible cuss (this was the south, remember?). And, his attention to detail? Better than anyone I had ever met. This BI-LO, Store 220 in West Columbia, was the largest volume store in the *chain for years. What does it take to run the highest volume store in the chain? **A pinpoint attention to detail.***

*I was in fear of our store walks each morning, as I had gradually been promoted to running the night stock crew. But, you know, after a while, it became a game- a challenge. I would finish my stocking load, and then walk the aisles before he came in. I was looking for everything he would see. The lesson? I know it's cliché, but **"retail is detail"** is true. The little things count when it comes to running a store. From building a strong team, to setting high standards, to keeping your night crew happy, they would all be formative lessons as I kept moving up the food chain (yes, food pun). I fully appreciated what Bob taught me about how to run a store and how to set your standards higher than all others.*

Through various management training programs, through meeting some people I would cherish the rest of my life, through getting off third shift just to go back on a year later, all while earning my Bachelor of Science degree from the University of South Carolina, I came to fall in love with the food industry.

When I graduated, I didn't go looking for the "real job" I had promised myself. I was there. I was hooked. Fast forward a bit, through stints of becoming one of the youngest Store Managers in the BI-LO chain (my first store- BI-LO 240 in Pineville, North Carolina), to running five stores for BI-LO (240 in Pineville, 242 on Park Road in Charlotte, NC, to 64 on Broad River Road in Columbia, SC to 33 on Beltline Road in Columbia to 270 on Dorchester Road in Charleston, South Carolina), I was forming a skill set that would become a base for the rest of my career.

I am a true believer that you will never be a strong merchant in the corporate office if you've never been an operator in the stores, where you have constant contact with those people handing you money, the customers. If you have not walked in the shoes of those for whom you are building your programs, you have no idea how they are going to be received or even executed. Besides, being an "operations guy" has a ton of credibility when you are eventually at the corporate office. No one ever forgets the nights you spent re-setting the store in Pageland, or the times you helped re-supply Charleston after Hurricane Hugo.

Then came The Partnering Group and the science called Category Management. Previously, the idea was grocery chains should carry a ton of items and let the customers have variety, variety, variety. Along comes Walmart, and the game changed to logistical and assortment efficiency and effectiveness. Then, a funny thing happened on the way to the Forum, the customer decided they wanted to play. In fact, they demanded that the retailer cater to their needs, not the other way around.

In essence, we had shifted from "marketing to" to "marketing with". The days of "this is what we have, convince them to buy it" were over. Quickly, the era of "what does the customer want, and how can we efficiently and effectively serve them" was taking hold. For more on Category Management, see my book Category Management Principles.

As The Partnering Group, and their lively energetic founder, Dr. Brian Harris, were taking over the industry, BI-LO (owned by Ahold at the time) was forming a Category Management team at its headquarters in Mauldin, South Carolina. I was working on a Master of Science in Management degree, and fit the criteria of operationally knowledgeable and able to work inside a structured category management department. I said "no", of course. Why would I want to give up a life of being my own boss in the stores, living in Charleston at the time, and doing my own thing 250 miles from headquarters? Besides, one of my favorite people in the industry, Stuart, was my District Manager. Why leave this? I had even started golfing….

Stuart, upon hearing I turned down Ron's (Vice President of Merchandising at the time) offer to come to corporate, sat me down, and basically said I was being an idiot. I loved Stuart's directness…. Not having to be called an idiot twice, I decided to take the job and move to Mauldin, South Carolina. One of the best moves I could have ever made. Stuart was right. To be on the cutting edge of a new science called Category Management was an experience I could never replace. Not only were the fundamentals something I could use the rest of my career, but I ended up teaching Category Management inside the Food Marketing Tracks at Siena College and at the State University of New York (SUNY) at New Paltz, where I formed the curriculum and even wrote the text book (with Dr. Brian Harris), and now I'm with the premier Food Marketing program in the country at Western Michigan University.

The Director of Category Management at the time, Mike, was a burly guy with a straight-line focus on what needed to be done to be the best in the industry. I learned a lot from Mike over the years, and still count him as a friend today. Like I said, it's a small industry. Be ethical, stand to your principles, and you will form life-long relationships where you know you both will do what you say, when you say it, no bending the rules. That's how you form relationships.

At the time, I had no idea why Mike spent so much time on the category definition part of the Category Management process. It was so frustrating, let's just get on with it! Guess what I teach today? **The category definition is the most important part of the process!** Do not go quickly through it. The definition determines resources to allocate, guidelines for who is involved and who is not, guardrails for what to include and what to leave out. Mike was right. Thanks, Mike. One more person along the way who set high standards and attention to detail. I'm starting to see a success pattern here.

As the story would unfold, I ended up with an opportunity to join the Fleming Companies as they were changing to Fleming Inc., relocating from Oklahoma City to Dallas, and centralizing the twenty-nine distribution centers from around the country into one Customer Support Center. If there is any place I could branch out and develop leadership skills to catapult me in my career, it was here. If you could shape chaos into order, this was the place for you.

Five promotions later, and as the doors closed for the last time, I had run merchandising, convenience stores, tobacco, pet food, and a variety of businesses that would be sizeable stand-alone companies on their own, but were just part of the massive $25 billion company servicing 3,000 stores from coast to coast, including export to the Caribbean as well as a full-line division in Hawaii. Along the way, I am honored to have met fantastic people! I count my years at Fleming as some of the most formative years of my career.

As the doors closed on Fleming, and the company was folded into C&S Wholesale Grocers, Associated Wholesale Grocers, and the customer base fled like cats when you call them, I moved on to Bozzuto's. A family-owned and led company, with a dynamic trio at the top. Their vastly different personalities just kind of worked for that company. The retailers truly appreciate their attention to the independents, IGA appreciates their focus on the brand, and the industry is a better place because of companies like Bozzuto's. Great people and great friends. If a retailer was out of one case of one item and needed it that day, they would drive that item to them. No questions asked. Their relationships with their retailers are as tightly bound as you can get.

Opportunity knocked a few more times before I

became a professor. I went to Canada and headed up merchandising and marketing for The North West Company, operating in eleven time zones (including 42 stores above the Arctic Circle) under the banners Cost U Less (Caribbean and South Pacific), Alaska Commercial (in….Alaska), Giant Tiger (southern Canada), Northern Stores (creatively named for the far north of Canada), and North Mart (designed to reflect an enhanced assortment tied onto the same creative "North"). And then, returned to the United States to Price Chopper, in Schenectady, New York, to head merchandising, marketing, loyalty, advertising, health and wellness, etc. All companies with great histories and excellent teammates.

Now, as a Marketing Professor and Director of the best Food Marketing program in the world at Western Michigan University, food is my default. It's where I go when a student wants an elaboration on a concept, it's where I go when someone wants to discuss how an industry can evolve, it's where I go because it is my comfort zone- my "happy place". Just a little history about a cool career in the food industry!

Made in the USA
Monee, IL
11 September 2023

42518947R10066